WRITE ON

HOW TO OVERCOME WRITER'S BLOCK SO YOU CAN WRITE YOUR NOVEL

L. M. LILLY

INTRODUCTION

The image of a writer staring at a blank screen or, if you're old school, a typewriter or blank sheet of notebook paper, is almost iconic. There's excitement there. And romance. Especially if there's an antique roll top desk in the picture.

But that image also can evoke fear. Fear of never filling that blank page or screen. Of being unable to conjure whole worlds and characters from nothing. Fear of writer's block.

Despite writing a book about overcoming it, I've never liked the phrase, which I find completely unhelpful. A block sounds solid and hard to get past. As if you literally can't write.

And that's not so. If you needed to write to save the life of someone you loved, I'm confident you would. At the very least, you'd write a grocery list or describe the plot of your favorite book. Or copy the first paragraph of this Introduction and scribble your thoughts about writer's block.

So the issue, short of injury or illness that prevents it, isn't that you can't write. But it might be any number of other things. Maybe you feel you can't write a novel. Or anything good enough to belong in a novel, whatever "good enough" means to you. It could be the critical voice in the back of your mind keeps whispering that you'll never be a great writer, so why try? Or maybe you rarely feel excited about writing. It's a slog, and you have so much else on your plate you just don't know if it's worth it. Except....you want to write a novel. Or finish the one you already started back when you were excited about it.

Which brings me to the other reason the phrase writer's block causes more, well, blocks. It suggests there's one answer to all of the above issues. Defeat writer's block in 3 easy steps! Wait – there's a great book to write.

Much as I wish I had a one-size-fits-all-writers answer, instead, there are many. To make it trickier, what works for me, or for another novelist, might not work for you. It might not even work for me next month because there could be a different reason I'm slowing down or stalling.

But there are ways to address the issues that make writing more challenging or lead to you feeling stuck or blocked. Lots of them. By the time you finish this book, odds are you'll have discovered quite a few that will help make writing easier and more fun. And will get you through the times when it's not.

Is This Book For You?

If you want to write a novel but are struggling to get started, wrote quite a few chapters and are stalling out as you approach the middle, or you keep rewriting and can't seem to get to the end, this book is meant for you. In addition to ways to simply get words flowing, it looks at larger issues that relate specifically to novels.

I aimed this book at novelists because much of the advice I've found out there on writer's block is generic. For example, store-bought writing prompts can be helpful, and Chapter 5 covers those. They can be great to spark an idea for a scene. But is it a scene I can use in my novel? Quite often not, and all the challenges of novel writing are still there.

So while other writers may find this book useful, most of it deals specifically with sorting out and addressing whatever is making it harder for you to write or finish a novel.

What This Book Includes (And Doesn't)

Part 1 focuses on getting a novel started. It addresses challenges you might be facing, including feeling stuck because you're unsure if you've found an idea broad and deep enough for a novel, questioning whether you need to plot in advance (spoiler – it depends), and getting past the need to write something perfect or, for that matter, good in your earliest draft.

In Part 2, we'll talk about keeping your momentum going through the middle of your novel, where a lot of writers find their enthusiasm, and their plots, faltering. Some of the issues covered include finding the best way to motivate yourself, engaging your unconscious mind to help you write more easily, and creating a writing routine – whether or not you can write every day. Also, staying excited throughout the process.

Finally, Part 3 covers finishing an entire draft of your novel. It starts with why it's important to do that even if you feel like (or are certain!) it's not "good." Then the book specifically addresses the hopes and fears many novelists share, particularly as they relate to success and failure, that can make it harder to cross the finish line. And, of course, ways to deal with those so you can regain your excitement and write until the end.

Throughout, the book also includes practical nuts-and-bolts tips and specific questions and exercises to help you tap into your creativity, have fun, and finish your novel.

What you won't find are instructions on crafting your entire plot, creating well-rounded characters, or dealing with other story elements. Those are important, and there are lots of books out there about them. (Including a few of my own, which are listed in Chapter 25.) This also isn't a How To guide to increase your daily or weekly word count, though you may find some of the chapters or exercises send you rocketing forward.

Finally, you won't find advice about becoming more disciplined and working harder. I'm sure you already do lots of things in your life that require discipline and hard work. If that's all you needed you wouldn't be reading this book. Instead, I hope this book will give you more insight into your own creative process so you can jumpstart your novel and write more freely and happily to the end.

How To Use This Book

While the book is organized around the beginning, middle, and end of the novel-writing process, nearly all the exercises and topics could be useful at any stage of your writing. The Part 1 chapters on finding ideas, for instance, can also help if you're feeling stuck at the halfway mark of your novel or struggling with what needs to happen at the climax. Likewise, you may find the exercises and questions in Part 3 about success, failure, and fear are most helpful as you're starting your novel or keep you going through the middle.

For that reason, I suggest reading the entire book once and highlighting or making notes about which chapters speak to you the most. You can then return and do the exercises. Of course, if a question or suggestion strikes you as immediately helpful on your first read, feel free to set this book aside and try it in the moment. Especially if you feel excited about it. If it sends you to your keyboard and you never come back, I won't be offended. And I'll still be here if you need a jumpstart again down the road or when you write your next novel.

As far as the questions and exercises go, you can write in a separate notebook, on your computer or phone, or in the workbook edition of this book. Or you can simply think them through, though personally I think it's ideal to write about them. It helps reinforce your writing habits and keep the words flowing.

A Few Words About Me

As I'm sharing a lot about novel writing and getting unstuck, you might want to know what novels I've written. I finished my first novel a year after I graduated college, where I majored in Writing/English. My fiction writing classes focused almost entirely on initial inspiration, writing quickly, and writing vivid scenes. At the time I felt frustrated that there was almost no discussion of plot or theme.

Looking back, though, I think I failed to appreciate how important it was to learn how to find ideas and spark creativity, as well as to write quickly and without fear. I credit my classes with why overall I feel less anxiety than most writers do about writer's block or getting stuck.

In 2011, I published my first novel, a supernatural thriller called *The Awakening.* (Not the one I finished right after college. That never saw the light of day.) There are three more books in the same series, which is now complete. Together, they've been downloaded over 100,000 times. They're also my best sellers. I wrote the first three while working 50-65 hours a week practicing law, so there were definitely barriers to writing and finishing.

My second fiction series is the Q.C. Davis Mystery series. These novels are traditional detective/female sleuth mysteries. Right now, I'm writing the fifth one. The series also includes a novella. The second mystery, *The Charming Man,* was a 2019 Wishing Shelf Book Awards finalist. Windy City Reviews called the fourth book, *The Troubled Man,* a classic Chicago mystery and said my protagonist is "relentless and clever and lets nothing stand in her way."

In addition, I wrote a gothic horror novel and a collection of 3 tales of urban horror, one of which was made into a short film.

If nothing else, I hope this list shows I'm able to write on and finish novels.

Okay, are you ready to get started? Read – and write – on.

PART I

STARTING YOUR NOVEL: IDEAS AND EARLY PAGES

1

THE ORDER OF WRITING WHAT YOU LOVE

If you want to have fun writing your novel and avoid getting stuck, one of the best places to start is the stages of the writing process. It splits roughly into six phases:

- Generating and sifting through ideas
- Planning, plotting, or shaping your story
- Writing early drafts
- Revising the story elements (such as plot, theme, and characterization)
- Line editing (for clarity, flow, and impact of specific words and sentences)
- Fine tuning and final proofreading

The Order Of Things

We'll talk about the first two in the next few chapters. But I deliberately didn't number these phases because most of us shift between them as we write. If you like to figure out your story by writing it, you may spend little or no time shaping or plotting your novel before your early drafts, but you'll likely do a lot of adjusting when you revise. And while some writers do all their idea sorting and imagining early, it's not unusual to revisit that stage later if a plot turn doesn't work or you add a new subplot.

Keeping some phases as separate as possible, though, will help you write more and write more quickly.

First, save the line editing and proofreading for the end. Otherwise you'll spend a lot of time and energy on each word and sentence in paragraphs, scenes, or entire chapters you may very well cut later. That's energy and excitement that you'll want to draw on for other stages of your novel.

Second, and most important for getting past any sort of writer's block, is to keep your early drafting phase separate from your revision process.

Why Not Revise?

This might be biggest issue I see with writers who never get their first novel finished or even well underway. If you start revising in depth before you finish an entire draft it's far too easy to be six months – or six years – down the road and have polished chapters but no novel. And you can't always see what's happening because after all, you're writing, and your scenes may well be improving with every pass through. But you're not writing a novel.

I'll say it again because if you take nothing else from this book, I want you to remember:

If you're rewriting your chapters again and again, you're writing, but you're not writing a novel.

You're writing chapters.

You're also using time and energy you could spend finishing your novel instead. I can't tell you how often I've reworked a scene from different points of view, or with more or less dialogue, or in a different setting, and finally, frustrated, left it and moved. Only to find when I finished a rough draft that the scene didn't work because it didn't need to be there.

The second reason to separate writing from drafting is that the part of our brain that revises – think of it as your editor – is highly critical. That's great when you revise because that's when you need to spot what needs work and address it. (Rather than being in love with your words and unwilling to improve.)

But it is absolutely the opposite of great when it comes to writing your early draft, and especially your very first pages. That editor voice (which for me sounds a lot like my mom) will question every word, every phrase, every character. It makes it almost impossible to get words on a page.

It makes us want to stop writing altogether rather than face the criticism we're sure our writing will draw.

Exceptions

There are a few exceptions to the No Revising Early advice. You may find you need to do a light edit of a previous scene to get your next scene rolling. This may be particularly useful if you sort out your plot by writing it or use a fairly loose structure as I do. So if a light revision helps you, go for it, but keep an eye on how many revisions. If you've revisited a scene 3 or 4 times, it's probably time to let it go and move on. You can make a note in brackets about what you think you'll need to change later, which might make you feel more comfortable continuing on.

Another exception is the one I mentioned in the Introduction, and it applies to everything in this book or any book on writing. What works for me or for many other writers may not work for you and vice versa. There are a small number of writers who do revise every scene until they're satisfied before they move on. Often those writers do next to no revisions. Essentially, they are writing a final draft from Day One.

If you're a newer writer, though, or you're having trouble with writer's block, you'll probably be better off finishing your entire draft first and then revising.

That can be hard because for most of us, the first draft of a scene is not up to our standards. The urge to fix it is strong. But you can get past that – and keep the drafting and editing phases separate – by giving yourself a simple instruction:

Write something bad.

Hemingway and Bad Writing

Most of us don't associate Ernest Hemingway with bad writing. Whether you like his fiction or not, he's known for his clean prose where every word counts. Yet you've probably heard that Hemingway said all first drafts are sh*t.

I firmly believe in that concept. I tell it to myself all the time. (It's also why no one but me ever sees my very first attempt at any type of writing.)

The fact is, like any skill, writing takes practice. Think about the other things you've learned to do. If you never cooked before in your life, did your first meal come out of the oven perfectly cooked and impeccably seasoned? If you're a teacher, did the students find you enthralling on your first day? When as a kid you got on a two-wheel bike did you ride away on Day One with no training wheels?

I'm guessing not. And while your first drafts will get better the more of them you write, a novel includes many moving parts that need to come together. Characters, a main plot, subplots, themes, descriptions, dialogue, and more. Insisting that you get all of that just right the first time through is a recipe for giving up, freezing at the keyboard, or a long slog of unhappy writing sessions.

And that's what we want to avoid. Because the more you enjoy writing your novel, the more likely you finish it. So let's talk for a moment about what you love about writing.

What You Love About Writing

I love writing novels. And I believe you do, too. Sure, there are days, maybe too many of them, that you don't feel that way, which might be part of why you picked up this book. But on some level, you love to write novels or you'd simply say forget it and find something else to do that you like better, or that's more apt to earn you money.

Focusing on what you love about writing can go a long way toward starting and finishing a novel. So take 15 or 20 minutes to write about exactly that. Be specific. For example, I love getting absorbed in new worlds and characters to the point where I forget everything else. It's a sort of Zen state that feels fabulous and draws on all parts of my brain.

Most often that happens when I'm shaping my ideas into a plot and imagining my characters, and when I do my first major revision. First drafting and fine tuning are less engaging for me and feel more like a slog. But I remember how fantastic I feel during the other parts and it carries me through.

Now that we've talked about the stages of novel writing and what you love about it, let's get to one of the biggest reasons many novelists struggle to get started – coming up with what they feel is a good idea for a novel.

Questions

- **What are the stages of the writing process?**
- **Which one do you enjoy the most?**
- **Which phases have you gotten stuck in before?**
- **Which one do you find the most fun?**

_____

_____

_____

_____

_____

_____

_____

_____

_____

_____

_____

_____

2

COMING UP WITH IDEAS FOR YOUR NOVEL

If you're staring at a blank screen, it may have nothing to do with being blocked or unable to write or write well. You might simply feel uncertain what your novel should be about. That uncertainty keeps many aspiring novelists from diving in. It sometimes stalls experienced authors as well. Which is likely why people so often ask writers where they get their ideas.

The good news is that the more novels you write the more ideas for them tend to appear, and the easier it is to evaluate which one will likely work for a full-length novel. Then the challenge becomes choosing one from among many, which I'll get to in Chapter 7.

If you're searching for ideas now, though, and feeling stuck, it's not much comfort to know it'll get easier down the road.

So let's talk about what it takes to come up with a good idea for a novel. If you've already got one, you can skip ahead, but you may want to read anyway. That way if you feel stuck later, you'll more quickly identify whether your idea (or lack of one) is the issue. And you'll know how to address it.

Raw Material, Relaxation, Refinement

Ideas come from a mix of raw materials, relaxation, and refinement.

The raw materials for a novel include everything that you experience, feel, sense, and learn. Often when we're stuck, we need raw materials beyond our day-to-day lives. Which is great news because there are lots of ways to give your mind more to work with. Or, to put it another way, to feed your creative mind.

Relaxation allows our brains to roam freely, imagine, and make connections that otherwise we miss. And refinement helps you put all of it together. Such as a childhood memory of rusty swing sets in a park, an article about the latest rocket launch, and a book you read about climate change that come together into an idea for a dystopian science fiction novel.

Sometimes this process happens unconsciously, other times you need to prompt it, which we'll talk more about in Chapter 7. For now, though, because finding raw materials often goes hand in hand with relaxation, we'll start there.

Questions

- **Do you have one or more ideas for a novel now?**
- **What ways do you already use to generate ideas?**
- **What does it mean to you to refine raw materials into an idea for a novel?**

_____
_____
_____
_____
_____
_____
_____
_____
_____
_____

L. M. LILLY

_____

_____

_____

_____

_____

_____

_____

_____

_____

_____

_____

_____

_____

_____

3

RELAX AND FEED YOUR CREATIVE MIND

Getting outside your usual physical surroundings often helps your mind relax and wander, generating ideas. The options for doing that work well for me and other writers I know, so you can give them a try or use them to inspire your own list. The key is to experiment. Because what works for me might not work for you.

Also, what generates ideas one time for you may not another time and vice versa. So if you return to this chapter again in the future, you may want to try one of these activities even if it didn't inspire you before.

Watch And Listen Live

Concerts and other live music events, plays and musicals, and sporting events can all be wonderful ways to relax and set your mind free.

Research shows listening to music lights up different parts of your brain than do most day-to-day activities. At the same time it stimulates your brain it can decrease blood pressure and help you relax. For me, live music especially sparks ideas. There's something about the energy of the crowd and the excitement and tension of the musicians, who in a way are doing a high wire act without a net.

Will they stay on key? Keep the rhythm steady? Remember the words?

That bit of tension can draw you into the drama, sounds, and sights, freeing you from the types of concerns that normally fill your mind. Even if you're listening or watching online or on a device, music can take you to another world. Simply experience it and let your mind drift rather than trying to come up with ideas.

Sometimes ideas swirl in my mind as I'm listening. Or when I leave a concert, suddenly I'm full of new story ideas. Other times they come to me days later while I'm doing something else. But live music in particular almost always triggers a story idea or sparks a scene or new character moment.

Watching live theater can have the same effect. The ways the actors say their lines, the set design, even the script itself can prompt new ideas for stories or twists on current projects. If you can't watch a live production, look for on-line recordings of live theater. You won't feel the same level of excitement and energy as you will when you're in the theater with the actors, but you'll get some of the effect.

If sports interest you (or even if they don't), watching a game in person or televised can help you lose yourself in the moment, which can trigger more ideas. The excitement or frustration of the crowd, the focus of the players. Choose a side to root for so you can experience the ups and downs. Or try out a new sport and see what you can learn from the announcers.

Whichever you do, your mind is apt to unwind and offer you some new ideas.

What's wonderful is it doesn't matter if you love music, the play, or the game, or dislike or hate them. Either way, they'll evoke feelings and possibly memories, both of which can lead to ideas.

Visual Art

Visual art is another wonderful way to relax and immerse yourself in an experience outside yourself. It also helps spark ideas because you're literally seeing a part of the world from another person's viewpoint.

So visit a museum and stare at a painting or sculpture. (If you happen to live somewhere, as I do, that features art in outdoors spaces or public buildings, those are great options, too.) Study the detail, the background, the colors, the shapes. If you can't go in person to view art, do the same with a full-color art book. No need to search for ideas or to love what you're seeing. Simply let it absorb you. Like music, visual art often sparks deep emotion or calls forth memories long forgotten.

Sounds Of Silence

During the many writing classes I took as a student at Columbia College in Chicago, our professors often instructed us to sit in complete silence. We listened first for sounds inside the classroom and the building. Next, because our windows opened onto Wabash Avenue, a busy street, we listened for outside sounds. After what felt like forever (but likely was fifteen minutes or so), we were directed to imagine a scene that fit a sound we heard.

After that we had about fifteen minutes to write what we'd imagined as fast as we could. Then we shared what we wrote.

That mix of concentrating on sounds and tapping into my imagination was surprisingly relaxing. It took me away from my day-to-day worries, which included paying tuition and other expenses, commuting late at night, and juggling work and school. The sounds I heard often sparked brand new story ideas. Other times I imagined a scene that became part of an ongoing project. And sometimes I wrote the scene for class and forgot it later. But it always got me writing.

A Change Of Place

A simple change of place can spark ideas and help you relax. It can be a big change, like flying or driving to a different country or state. Or a minor relocation like walking in a large park if you're live in a busy, noisy city.

Altering your routine in a minor way can do the same for you. Walk down a street or around a block outside your usual route. The key is to do it deliberately and pay attention. What do you notice about the buildings, trees, or landscape around you? Are there sounds you don't normally notice? New smells (pleasant or not)?

Pick a small area to study. Look at how the light hits it, how many shades of colors are in the grass or the concrete. Focus on details and let go of your daily life. Odds are, when you return home you'll feel refreshed and will have some new ideas.

Move Your Body

Physical movement often sparks creativity all on its own. I find taking a walk and talking through ideas in my head or out loud (if no one's around that I'll be bothering) can make a huge difference. If I can't walk outside, I'll pace in my condo or climb the stairs. Sometimes after a yoga session I magically know what I want to write. Joe Lallo on the podcast 6 Figure Author mentioned he likes juggling or walking in circles.

Books, News, And Documentaries

What you read affects how far your mind can range. (This also applies to listening if you take in content that way.) And reading outside of your usual patterns works best for sparking ideas.

If you never read about scientific discoveries, pick up a book about one. I rarely read biographies or memoirs. But during Covid lockdowns I read books about three different presidential candidates in the United States. One of them I campaigned for, one I disagreed with but respected, and another I thought was awful while in office. Reading about each, and sometimes about the same moment in history from their different perspectives, fascinated me. While none of it directly relates to the novel I'm writing now, already I have in mind character moments and ideas for future projects.

You can also try reading novels of a type you don't normally read. The goal isn't to figure out how to write that genre or imitate it. Rather, it's to dive into a different fictional world, writing style, and type of character, which unconsciously will set your own mind spinning in new directions.

Watching documentaries can feed your mind and spark ideas, too. Choose a documentary on any topic that interests you, including ones you never plan to include in your writing. You might be surprised how many ideas start popping into your head as you watch or in the days and weeks that follow.

The Beauty Of Print

It's old school, but when sparking ideas reading in print can be far better than reading on a device. For one thing, many of us connect being in front of a laptop, tablet, or phone with fiction writing and other types of work, and the idea is to step away from both. Also, studies show that when we read online our minds tend to look for the next link to click. That makes it harder to get lost in what we're reading, allowing our minds to relax and roam freely.

Trying any or all of these activities should help you come up with ideas for your novel. You can also draw from your daily life, which we'll talk about in the next chapter.

~

Questions

- Which of the suggestions in this chapter appeals to you most?
- Have any of them sparked ideas in the past?
- What can you do or where can you go this week to take in art, music, or culture?
- Are there topics that interest you but that you don't know all that much about?
- What are they?
- How can you learn more?

_____

_____

_____

_____

_____

_____

_____

_____

_____

_____

_____

_____

_____

_____

_____

_____

_____

_____

_____

_____

_____

_____

_____

4

IDEAS FROM YOUR LIFE

Your life can also spark ideas. But often you need to look at it in a new way – sometimes more closely, sometimes from a different perspective – for that to happen.

Here are some ideas about how to go about that.

Your Work

Knowledge and experience from another job or profession can provide an entire backdrop for your novel. Authors like Scott Turow and John Grisham used their experiences as lawyers to create exciting novels and sparked what was a new genre at the time, the legal thriller.

But that's not the only way to mine your work experience for ideas. If you don't want to write about the ins and outs of your profession, your main characters may not share your work background. But one of your side characters might. Or the way someone at work speaks or interacts with others might inspire a character who works at something else but shares certain qualities with your coworker.

Also, even mundane aspects of your work can send your mind in new directions if you're paying attention. Much of my work as a lawyer involves lawsuits over insurance policies. Doesn't sound too exciting, does it? (It's okay, I accept that.)

In passing a client mentioned something called a suicide clause in a life insurance policy. It's a term that says if the policyholder commits suicide too soon (often two years) after buying the policy, it doesn't pay out.

This rattled around in my mind as a potential clue in a mystery. What if someone who worked in insurance and so knew all about this policy term, and had a son he loved dearly who depended on him for support, supposedly committed suicide months after buying life insurance? Insurance that was the only way to leave his son anything because the man's finances were otherwise in shambles?

Eventually this sparked the story that became my first female sleuth novel. The sleuth's boyfriend is about to move in with her, but the night before the move she finds him dead in his apartment. The police call it suicide, but one of many reasons she doesn't believe that's so is the suicide clause.

Reading About The World Around You

Real life events can also spark thought-chains of ideas. I started reading the Wall Street Journal when I opened my own law practice solely because I took few business classes in college and wanted to better understand my corporate clients. But I quickly found it helped my fiction writing by sparking ideas for novels, plot twists, and characters.

I find reading articles rather than watching newscasts work the best. That's because television news tends to focus on headlines and provide little more than sound bites about the topic. But the headlines that shout are more often the types of issues that come to mind anyway without paying attention to the news. What generates ideas are the details buried on page 3. Or, for that matter, the stories that start on page 10 or 20 (or the equivalent if you're reading online).

For example, years ago I read an article about scientists who isolated a gene that might allow certain species to live 1,000 years.

The question of whether such a gene could be inserted into a human intrigued me, though I don't write science fiction.

I was, though, writing *The Unbelievers*, the second book in my *Awakening* supernatural thriller series. The article prompted me to include a prophecy about The One Who Will Live Forever. In an early draft, that prophecy referred to a child my protagonist conceived in a supernatural way. Genetic testing revealed the child had that 1,000-year gene. That gene didn't make it into the final version of the book. It turned out to be a distraction — one too many threads for the reader to follow. But the prophecy remained, just with a different meaning. Had I not read the article I wouldn't have thought of it at all.

When reading news, you're not looking to take an idea directly and write about it (unless you liked "ripped from the headlines" plots). It's that a news story can be a springboard for an idea. Which means the more you take in and explore, the more you'll discover what to write about.

Listening To Others

Another great place to find ideas is through day-to-day conversations. The next time you talk to a friend, family member, or coworker, practice listening. So often during a conversation we rush to say what's on our minds. Instead, set aside your own concerns. Focus on what the other person says. Ask questions to encourage that person to share more about the issue, the feelings it prompts, and the circumstances around it.

If you find it hard to do that, try taking a breath after you think the other person has finished talking rather than starting to speak yourself. That allows the other person to finish a thought or elaborate on an idea. (And if your conversation partner has truly finished, it will make the conversation more relaxed and comfortable for both of you.)

I'm not suggesting that you put these conversations directly into one of your novels. As I talk about more below, aiming to do that might inhibit your writing and upset people you don't want to upset. If you're like me, though, you'll find that bits and pieces of what you hear from others spark ideas about conflicts you can then change or exaggerate. Also, you'll start finding it easier to imagine characters whose feelings, experiences, and views differ from your own.

And the more people whose points of view you truly listen to and understand the more characters and situations you'll start to imagine.

When Strangers Talk

I'm also a fan of listening to conversations of strangers out on the street, on the train, or in a crowded coffee shop. I don't sneak up on people and eavesdrop (though I admit sometimes I'm tempted). But often on crowded sidewalks in Chicago where I live, on trains, and in restaurants people talk to each other or on their phones right next to me. It's impossible not to hear. So rather than feeling constantly annoyed, I listen.

As with day-to-day conversations you have with people you know, overheard conversations are great sources of ideas for stories. As a bonus, you'll develop a better and better ear for other people's speech patterns, which helps with dialogue writing.

Different People, Different Views

If it's possible at your job, work with someone you don't usually partner with. If you're home with your children, see if you can get together with other parents or caregivers you don't normally interact with. Likewise, when you do have time to meet somebody for lunch or coffee, make it someone you haven't seen in quite a while. If you normally watch a particular news or commentary show because it lines up with your way of looking at the world, pick one with a completely different point of view.

Better yet, talk to someone whose views are completely opposite to your own and really listen. Don't argue. Just listen. If social media is your way to winding down at the end of the day or connecting with friends, visit some pages you rarely go to. Look at the photos. Read the posts and comments. Get a sense of how other people see the world.

A Few Caveats

Drawing too much from real life poses a few perils. Sometimes fictionalizing real-life experiences makes writing more vivid. But it also may leave you feeling anxious you'll reveal too much about yourself or the people around you, who might be upset or offended. Being uneasy about any of those things can make it harder to write.

Just as important, sticking too closely to reality limits what your fictional characters might do or what plot twists you imagine. Usually the farther you stray from "real life" the more your creative mind roams in new and interesting ways.

So even if you're writing autobiographical fiction, shake things up. Throw in a completely unfamiliar character, setting, or plot twist. Or stick with the facts in your first draft, reminding yourself that when you revise you can alter character aspects and experiences to make them unrecognizable to others, much the way some creative non-fiction writers do to protect identities.

If you're not aiming for autobiographical, focus instead on life experience as a jumping off point. A coworker's minor fear of heights, for instance, might prompt you to write a literary novel about a skydiver gradually losing her nerve or a thriller about mountain climbers caught in an avalanche.

Okay, we've talked about seeking outside experiences, like attending a symphony or wandering in the woods, and paying attention to your life experience. Sometimes, though, it can help to do things more specifically designed to spark ideas. Those things are otherwise known as writing prompts, which is what the next chapter covers.

Questions

- **Describe one conversation with someone that prompted a potential story or novel idea.**
- **Does anyone in your day-to-day life have a trait or**

manner of speaking that you'd love to borrow for a
character in a novel?
- Name a hope or fear someone you know has that you
  might exaggerate and use for a plot or subplot.

_____

_____

_____

_____

_____

_____

_____

_____

_____

_____

_____

_____

_____

_____

_____

_____

_____

_____

_____

_____

_____

_____

5

WRITING PROMPTS

Prompts for writers come in all types of formats, including books, calendars, decks of cards, and magnets. You can also create them for yourself. Most are not designed specifically to prompt ideas for novels. But you can still use them to imagine conflicts that can spark novel ideas.

Prompts For Sale

Many prompts give you a conflict, situation, or one or more characters (or all of the above) to start a story. For example, a woman carrying a small, noisy dog gets stuck in an elevator with a claustrophobic man. Or a boy steals a kite from his sister.

Others involve a setting and ask about your own life to prompt you to write a journal entry or description. You can also buy cards with words on them. I have a set of magnets, each with a word on it, that a friend brought me as a hostess gift for one of my New Year's Eve parties. Each magnet bears a single word. You choose five at random and use them in a scene or write about the ideas they spark.

These days I'm not a huge fan of these types of prompts because I usually have a novel underway that I prefer to focus on. (Which is why I'm considering creating a writing prompts book geared specifically toward those planning, writing, or revising a novel.)

But that doesn't mean that pre-made writing prompts can't work for you. Whether or not the scenes, descriptions, or character sketches you write become part of a novel, they get words flowing by giving you a place to start. You may use them as backstory or as prompts for exploring larger conflicts that turn into a novel.

Create Your Own

You can create your own writing prompts by typing or printing on slips of paper or index cards. On each one write a two, three, or four word basic description of a person, such as "old woman," "little boy," "angry person." Write two slips for each, so that you can use the same description more than once in the same session. Fold them so you can't see what's printed and set them aside.

Now create slips for verbs. On each slip print a verb that requires action, such as run, jump, hit, play, touch, throw, or swim. (You only need one of each.) Fold those so you can't read them.

Now draw one person, one verb, and another person and put them together, adding prepositions if necessary to create a basic sentence. Here are some examples:

- Angry man runs into little boy.
- Middle-aged woman skips with middle-aged woman.
- Little girl throws little boy.

As you write you can add nouns. Suppose your slip say this: "Little girl throws middle-aged man." You might use that as is and have fun figuring out how that little girl is going to throw a grown man. Or you might add an object: "Little girl throws spaghetti at middle-aged man."

These prompts are almost guaranteed to generate conflict, which is the key to a good plot.

Write for fifteen or twenty minutes about that conflict. Remember, you don't need to love the scene you write. In fact, if you don't you may shift gears entirely as you discover what you do love to write about. It's all about getting words on a page and, as you do, potentially prompting new ideas or bringing together threads that may become part of your novel. (Use the pages at the end of the chapter if you like.)

Borrow

You can also choose the first line from a favorite book (of any type) or a headline from a news article. As fast as you can, write four or five pages of a scene with that line or headline or about any ideas it generates.

As with the slips of paper, if you write a scene or scenes they may not end up in your novel. But it should get you writing. If you do use a scene, of course you'll need to change that first line later. You can borrow the words of other writers to prompt ideas, but you can't copy them and use them as if they're your own in your fiction.

Images

Decks of cards with images can prompt all sorts of ideas. Over the years I've used cards artists designed to help get in touch with the unconscious mind, an Angel card deck a friend bought me, and Tarot cards. I don't believe any of these cards have prophetic powers (though it's fine if you do), but the images gave me ideas.

All you need to do is take out a card at random. Study it for at least five minutes. (Set a timer to be sure you give yourself this time.) If you start thinking about other things, gradually bring your focus back to the card. Look at its colors. Contemplate the lines. Now write as much as you can as fast as you can for fifteen minutes about the image or images or any thoughts the images spark.

You can do the same thing with a group of two or three cards you look at together.

Pictures in print magazines can also work well to spark ideas. If you don't subscribe to print magazines anymore, check used bookstores or secondhand stores or ask friends if they have back issues to loan you. Looking at one image can spark ideas.

While you can look at images online, there's something about images on paper or cards that you can handle that helps you relax and sparks ideas.

Writing Exercises

Finally, you can try some exercises. You'll recognize the first one from my college days.

Listening: Sit in silence for fifteen minutes (set the timer again). Listen to every sound and let your mind wander. If you've already started a novel or have an overall idea for one, imagine how this sound fits into that idea. If not, simply free associate. What or who caused the sound? Imagine how everything smells, tastes, and feels, too. If your mind wanders that way, make up a scene or story to go with what you hear. When the fifteen minutes ends, reset the timer for the same amount. Now, as fast as you can and without lifting your pen from the page, write out everything you heard and imagined.

Collaging: Remember those old magazines you collected? Cut out lots of images from them (it doesn't matter what images or whether you like them), toss them into a box, mix them up, then take ones that speak to you out. Arrange them however you like and paste them into a collage. As you do, forget why you're doing this and just enjoy sorting and cutting and pasting. This process helps engage another part of your mind and let go of any concerns you feel about writing.

When you're done, look at the collage as a whole and the image in the center of it. How do you feel when you look at? What's the story that goes with it? If there's a place, what's happening there right now? If there's a person, what does that person do each day? How do they feel?

Write for fifteen minutes, answering one or more of these questions.

Scents: Take a walk and notice any smells around you. Or gather items in or around your home with strong odors – anything from scented candles to grass clippings to coffee grounds, obviously avoiding anything toxic or that you're allergic to.

Choose one, shut your eyes, and inhale. Does it trigger a memory? A feeling? Do you associate it with a particular time and place? If you have characters in mind for your novel, choose one of them and imagine this person smelling that scent. How does the character feel? React?

Write for fifteen or twenty minutes about that.

Any of these prompts can spark an idea for a scene, a character, or an entire novel. The goal isn't to be wedded to any one of those happening, though. As with the activities in the previous chapters, you want to relax and let your thoughts flow, then see what ideas come to mind for a novel.

But how do you move from getting the ideas flowing to forming them into an idea for a novel? That's the refinement part of the process. Which is what the next chapter is about.

Questions

- **Which type of prompt would you most like to try?**
- **Have you used any of these prompts in the past?**
- **Which ones?**
- **What ideas did they prompt?**

_____

_____

_____

_____

_____

_____

_____

_____

_____

_____

Try one of the writing prompts or exercises:

_____

_____

_____

_____

_____

_____

_____

_____

_____

_____

_____

_____

_____

_____

_____

_____

_____

_____

_____

_____

_____

_____

_____

6

BRINGING THE STRANDS TOGETHER

The ways of generating ideas we talked about in Chapters 3 and 4 involved taking in raw materials by broadening your experiences or what you pay attention to. Now you need to refine all of it into an idea for a novel. That often occurs when what you know or learn about a topic that fascinates you crosses over into another unrelated area of interest. Or when you hone in on a very specific aspect of a larger idea. Sometimes this process happens spontaneously. Other times you need to do it purposefully.

Along with some examples, I'll share some methods that might help you move forward.

Crossing Over

For years as I was establishing my law practice I thought about writing a novel on a *Rosemary's Baby* type of theme. It's a classic horror novel of the type I enjoy, based on quietly-building suspense and weaving in supernatural aspects without gore. Separately during that same time, I read a lot of books on the origins of religion, goddess lore, and female-focused spirituality. I wasn't looking for an idea for fiction when I delved into those types of books. A friend suggested them when I confided that I felt alienated by the religion I'd grown up in.

Then the book *The Da Vinci Code* came out. As you may remember, it was wildly popular. While many readers commented on it being a page-turner, nearly every woman I talked to loved the way the book explored a female-focused aspect to early Christianity.

That's when, after years of reading and thinking, I "suddenly" had an idea. I decided to write about a college girl, not religious, who didn't want to risk pregnancy before she got into medical school and chose to refrain from sex. But she suddenly discovers she's pregnant all the same. (The Rosemary's Baby aspect of the book's plot.) Her family members, best friend, and boyfriend don't believe she never slept with anyone. The only person who does believe her belongs to a powerful fringe religious cult. The cult sees the protagonist as the mother of a future messiah – until they learn her child will be a girl. That's the *Da Vinci Code* part of the inspiration. Then they turn on her, convinced she'll trigger the Apocalypse and she must be eliminated.

It felt almost magic to me, that moment that all of it came together.

If you're thinking, hey, wait, I don't want to wander around for years waiting for this process to happen, don't worry. Most of that process was unconscious for me because it happened when I had a busy law practice, then started my own law firm, and was finishing another novel (one I never published). But you can more purposefully sort out ideas for novels.

Sorting And Narrowing

Sometimes refining an idea means starting smaller. In *Zen and the Art of Motorcycle Maintenance* the narrator talks about advising a student who can't get started on an essay about the United States. He suggests instead she write about the town where she's living. She keeps returning for more advice, still stuck. The narrator, growing irritated, finally tells her to write about a specific building, then to write about a particular brick in that building.

At last, the student writes line after line, page after page.

Why? Because when you start with an idea that's broad, like the United States, you often get stuck because it's too soon to write. You don't truly know yet what to write about. Even the topic of a town could encompass almost anything, including the town's history, its government, the local store on the corner, a dispute between neighboring homeowners, or the town council's agenda from last week or last year or twenty years ago. But once she focused on one brick in a building, she could write.

As a novelist, you need to find or choose a brick. As with my supernatural thriller example, your unconscious mind might do that as you're busy with the rest of life. But you can also narrow it purposely.

When I was nearing the end of my supernatural thriller series (the first series I published) I spent time some time sorting through what type of series to write next. The first two items in the bullet point list below I chose based on what I most enjoyed reading at the time. But I narrowed it with the remaining items before I started sketching out my plot and writing.

- Mystery or suspense (general genre)
- In a Chicago setting (adding the setting)
- A female private investigator/detective novel (narrowing genre)
- The main character is a lawyer (protagonist)
- She used to be an actress – maybe as a child (protagonist back story)
- Her parents named her after one of her sisters, who died (back story – emotional pain)
- That sister, who was kidnapped and killed before the protagonist was born, also was a child actress and family favorite (more protagonist back story that provides motivation to investigate crimes)
- The key question of the first book is suicide or murder? (general plot – this is where that suicide clause popped back into my mind)
- She finds her boyfriend dead (motivation for protagonist – heart of plot)

- Long ago her parents were wrongly accused of her sister's murder (more motivation)

That process, most of it purposeful, took my general idea of writing a mystery or suspense novel set in Chicago to: "A mystery where a Chicago lawyer, who used to be an actress, discovers her boyfriend's dead body the night before they plan to move in together. The police say it's suicide, but she refuses to believe it and does her own investigation to uncover the truth." Plus before I wrote I knew some key parts of the main character's back story.

Though I did think about refining my idea, I didn't put the points above into a bullet list. (Despite that I am quite a fan of lists.) Many of them first occurred to me as I did the types of activities I described in Chapter 3, and I did a lot of free writing to bring them together, which I'll talk more about in a moment.

While you may not need quite as much detail to start writing, you can see that a general idea about genre tells little about where to start, what will happen, who the characters are, or what the results will be. Which can lead to staring at a blank screen with no idea how to move forward.

But as you narrow and refine your general idea you'll discover a lot about what will happen, where it will happen, who is involved, etc., making it far easier to write. Knowing the points in that bullet list gave me a pretty good start on early scenes of my first mystery *The Worried Man*. And some clues about running subplots for the series as well.

Letting the refinement process simply happen in your mind is a great option if you're at a time in your life when your schedule is overwhelming. But if you're actively looking to start a novel, you can refine by writing.

Write Your Way

Writing about your ideas is a great way to narrow and refine. You can ask and answer questions in writing about what you love to read and write and why. (Very meta, I know, but it works.) Ask yourself if you'd enjoy writing a novel in a particular genre, then write as much as you can about why or why not. Answer questions about what sorts of characters appeal to you, ways different topics you've read about or conversations you've overheard could come together into a novel, and what types of plots or characters you think are most fun to write about.

You can also start out with the phrase *What if* and write about different possibilities based on whatever thoughts your different activities sparked. These *What ifs* don't need to be fully formed ideas. For my mystery series, one of my *What ifs* was "What if I wrote about a lawyer?" I spent a lot of pages sorting through how I felt about that. Earlier in my career when I typically worked 6 days a week, the last thing I wanted was to write about law. I needed to sort out what it meant to me to tap into that part of my life and whether I'd enjoy it.

Plan to toss out or delete these pages or store them somewhere you likely won't go to again. That frees you to answer your questions and sort through your thoughts more freely. Nothing's set in stone. So explore that idea you think might go nowhere or might not be marketable. Consider that genre you never imagined you'd write.

The great thing about refining through writing is that at the same time you're getting into the habit of writing more and more. Which makes it that much easier to keep the words flowing when you do choose an idea.

The Way You Write

One way to help this process along is to change the tools you use. If you normally type into your laptop or desktop, buy a notebook and pen and write as fast as you can by hand instead about one or another of your trains of thought.

Why fast and why by hand? For me, writing quickly basically becomes a scrawl I find hard to decipher later, meaning no one else will ever be able to read it. As with planning to toss out pages, the scribbling frees me to explore ideas my mind might otherwise reject as being too boring, too out there, too confusing, etc., before I type a single word.

Using a pencil rather than a pen can also prompt new combinations of ideas. It brings me back to childhood when I imagined and wrote and created with far fewer limits and concerns than my adult brain imposes.

Another option is to dictate ways your ideas or research about different topics might cross. Most word processing programs include a function for dictating. You also can buy a program or app for it or try free online software like Google Docs. If you have a smartphone, look for the microphone icon on your keyboard. Open an email to yourself, click the microphone, and talk. You can then email it to yourself and save the email or cut and paste into a document. Or just leave it as is. The point is to get your mind spinning, not to save output in a particular form. You might never look at it again.

To make it easier, pace in your living room or outside and talk through ideas out loud.

It's not that any one method is better than another. It's that a change in routine will help you bring trains of thoughts together into novel ideas.

By now many ideas are likely forming in your mind. Which brings us to the issue covered in the next chapter. Sometimes you get stuck because rather than no ideas, you have too many.

Questions

- **What fiction genres do you most often read?**
- **If you're not a genre reader, describe the storylines of your two favorite mainstream or literary novels.**
- **Is there a particular type of protagonist that appeals to you?**
- **When you sought out raw materials, what three topics that you learned or thought about fascinated you the most?**
- **What's one plot that could draw on two of them?**

_____

_____

_____

_____

_____

_____

_____

_____

_____

7

CHOOSING ONE IDEA FROM MANY

Ironically, just as having no ideas can lead to staring at a blank screen, so can having lots of them. You may feel unsure which idea will keep a reader engaged for an entire novel. Or fear that you will lose interest in the idea halfway through. Another question is whether the idea will interest not only potential readers but editors or agents if you're trying to sell your writing to a traditional publisher.

These types of concerns can make it harder to write. For one thing, the second you imagine a scene or write a line, you may wonder if a different idea would work better. Some writers feel paralyzed, afraid of choosing the "wrong" idea. Or at least one they'll spend a lot of time on but later discard.

This chapter covers ways to choose from various ideas.

But first, and this sounds obvious but is easy to forget, you can write more than one novel. Also, an idea for a novel that doesn't quite work might become a short story or a novella. Or it might turn out to be backstory for a character that makes the novel you eventually write richer. Which means you can relax. You're not picking the one and only idea. Just the one you want to focus on right now.

What Makes A Novel

One approach is to pick an idea at random, start writing, and see how it goes. Some writers like the freedom that allows. If you're having trouble getting started, though, or it makes you feel anxious (as it does me) to write without a bit of planning, taking time to consider which ideas lend themselves to the broad scope of a novel can make it far easier to start a novel.

While there are lots of elements to a novel, the following are ones I've found useful to look at when sorting through ideas:

- Conflict
- Characters
- Time Frame
- Subplot(s)
- Settings
- Points of View

No one of these factors tells you which novel idea will work best for you. But each is worth considering if you're trying to choose among several potential storylines.

Conflict

As I talk about in my book *Super Simple Story Structure: A Quick Guide To Plotting And Writing Your Novel*, without conflict there's no story. If your main character gets everything she wants and has a lovely day, there's no story, let alone a plot for a novel. Your protagonist must desperately want something and need to overcome obstacles to get it. And if you're writing a novel, the conflict needs to be large enough and the obstacles significant enough that it will take your protagonist the entire length of the book to reach a resolution.

So the first question to ask yourself is which of your ideas involves the most conflict?

Some ideas spark enough conflict and create enough questions to fill a novel or perhaps a series of them. Others lend themselves to a quicker resolution. If you try to base a novel on one of those you often end up stretching, filling, or padding your scenes with unnecessary dialogue, twists that don't truly matter, and lengthy description, which rarely makes for compelling reading.

A novel for an adult usually runs at least 45,000 or 50,000 words on the short side and upwards of 100,000 words on the long side, depending on genre. If this is your first novel, it may be hard to estimate whether your conflict will sustain that length. The best way is to review a few novels in the general genres you're thinking of. See how long each one is and how much the protagonist must do to reach the end of the novel.

By looking at how the conflicts in those novels compare to the ones that relate to your ideas, you can start to get a sense of what might work best.

The remaining factors will also help you decide if your conflict is large enough.

Timeframe

A novel can take place in a short timeframe, such as a day or a week, or span months, years, decades, or generations. That can be true of short story as well, so merely the time period doesn't weigh on one side or the other.

But the more scenes you imagine taking place in each block of time, whether it's an hour or a generation, the more likely your idea will sustain a novel.

Characters

The total number of characters doesn't tell you that much one way or the other about the scope of your idea. A short story usually includes, at most, a handful of characters. Or perhaps only one character, such as where a human being faces nature or a machine as the antagonist.

In contrast, novels can include dozens of characters because there is time and space for readers to become engaged with them. But some novels, like short stories, feature a fairly small cast of characters. And there are novels that feature just one character.

If your idea, however, requires you to delve in to the inner lives, motives, emotions, and background of more than a few characters, or needs an in depth development of one or two characters, it likely will work well for a novel. That's because the most engaging plot won't grab a reader if there's no reason to care what happens to the characters. A novel gives you space to develop each key character as a person. An idea that requires that to work lends itself to a good novel.

Subplots

Most short stories have one plot and only one plot, and it's about the main characters. While that plot may have several layers, there usually isn't room for much in the way of side stories. Novels, in contrast, almost always feature a main plot and more than one subplot. Subplots can include side stories for main characters or plots for secondary characters.

For instance, in *The Girl On The Train*, the main plot is solving the crime the protagonist believes she's witnessed. Subplots include her relationships with her ex-husband and the friend she's staying with, as well as her internal struggles with self-esteem and alcohol dependency.

As another example, the plot in *Pride and Prejudice* follows protagonist Elizabeth and her relationship with Darcy. A very well-developed subplot, though, occurs between Elizabeth's sister Jane and Bingley. That subplot gets almost as much space in the novel as the main plot. In addition, the novel features subplots about Elizabeth's younger sister Lydia, her father's realizations about himself, and her friend Charlotte, all of which both intertwine with the main plot and stand on their own.

While you don't need to know all the potential subplots to decide if your idea will work for a novel, if it makes you think of related conflicts that sound like compelling subplots you'd love to write, that's ideal.

Settings

As with timeframe, a short story often features only a handful of settings. In contrast, novels often include many locations. Some use different buildings or outdoor spaces in a single town or city, others range across a country, the world, or more than one world. With enough conflict, a novel can take place in one or two settings, so don't automatically discard that type of idea. But a larger number of settings can help keep you and readers engaged for the long haul.

Point Of View

Most short stories are told from one character's point of view and focus on what happens to that character. In contrast, while a novel typically includes only one protagonist, often quite a few characters' lives, minds, and feelings are explored. In fact, some characters might have their own stories that intersect with the protagonist's, but only in peripheral way. Readers often become great fans of side characters and may finish your novel as much to see what happens to them as to the protagonist.

This can be so even in novels the protagonist narrates. My third Q.C. Davis mystery (*The Fractured Man*), for example, is told in first-person but includes blog posts a suspect wrote about her father and the cult-like self-improvement company he belongs to. And in all the Q.C. Davis mysteries, protagonist Quille interviews people in depth, which gets across each one's point of view through dialogue. In that way, I'm able to tell multiple stories within Quille's narrative of solving crimes.

In fact, the length of novels almost demands that you include in one way or another the point of view of multiple characters. So if you're undecided, you may want to lean toward the idea that includes more than one character whose viewpoint you long to explore.

What's Love Got To Do With It?

While all the elements above provide some clues to whether your idea will work well for a novel, the most important is whether you'll enjoy writing it.

No matter how fast you write, writing a novel takes many, many hours. Depending on what else is on your plate, you may live with this story for months or years. And there will be times, no matter how intriguing your story is, that your interest will flag. Which is all the more reason to start with an idea that truly excites you and that you'll enjoy writing about for a long time to come.

Marketing And Sales

Many writers hope to earn money writing novels, or at least to reach a significant number of readers. But focusing too much on what's likely to sell when you choose your idea can make writing harder, especially for a first novel. That's so because now in addition to learning to create compelling characters and plots, write dialogue, weave in themes, and pay attention to pacing, you're also trying to predict sales.

Which is an entirely separate learning curve.

That being said, if you're sorting through ideas you're equally excited about and that you feel will all work for a novel, you could look for an overlap between sales potential and what you love. Imagine drawing one circle that includes all the genres, topics, or ideas you're excited about, and another that includes the ones that are easiest to sell. If an idea falls into the area where those two circles overlap, why not choose that one?

To shift to the other side of the fence again, one reason not to do that is that no matter how fast you write, odds are when you're ready to sell your novel the top of the bestseller list (whichever one you look at) will look very different than it does now. Also, sometimes you'll find it easier to sell a book with a small but devoted following rather than a book in the most popular genre.

In short, if you want to consider marketing, especially if you have many ideas that excite you, go ahead and do that. If it tends to make you freeze, causes you worry, or will require many extra hours of research before you start writing, you'll have a better chance of starting and finishing your novel without getting stuck if you let it go.

Now that you've chosen an idea – and if you haven't, the exercise at the end of this chapter may help – it's time to start writing. Or, maybe, plotting, which is what the next chapter is about.

Idea Exercise

Make a list of your ideas for a novel. Pick one at random, set a timer for 20 or 30 minutes (yes, I love timers), and write a scene, any scene that could happen anywhere in the novel.

If you don't have a scene in mind, write about the idea itself, starting with "What if." For example, you might write "What if a young woman training for the Olympics becomes catastrophically injured? How would she handle it?" Then start brainstorming, on paper, aloud, or on your keyboard, about what that woman might do, what her goals might be, and obstacles she'd face. Think about the other characters she'll meet and whether they will help or hinder her.

_____

_____

_____

_____

_____

_____

_____

_____

_____

_____

_____

_____

_____

_____

_____

_____

_____

_____

_____

_____

_____

Next time you have 20 or 30 minutes, try another idea, and so on.

Once you've written about a few ideas, ask yourself how excited you feel about each. Then go back to the factors talked about in this chapter. Which ideas strike you as best suited to a novel?

Wherever your excitement and the factors cross over, you've probably found a good idea for your novel.

If the idea you're most excited about doesn't seem like it will work well based on the elements discussed in this chapter, no need to abandon it. Spend some more time free writing about it with an eye toward how you might expand or change it until you feel more sure it will sustain a novel.

Can you give the protagonist a bigger goal? Add more obstacles? More locations? A stronger antagonist (the character whose reason for being is to thwart the protagonist)?

If none of the ideas works, go back to the previous chapter and start generating more ideas.

8

PLOT OR NOT?

As you probably guessed by now, I talk a lot about ideas because so often the stuck feeling you get when sitting at the keyboard isn't about the writing process, it's about not knowing what to write. Or to write next. That's especially true with novels. My novels average about 330 pages in paperback or around 75,000-85,000 words. That means a lot of writing sessions, a lot of scenes, and a lot of chapters.

Which raises the question: Is it easier to write if you know what's going to happen all the way through?

Like so many aspects of writing, there's no one answer to that question. Each writer is different. Also, different approaches may work at different stages of your writing career and life. Finally, whether to plot your novel before you write isn't a yes-or-no question. There are writers who don't plot at all and those who write detailed, lengthy outlines, but there are lots of in-between options as well.

All of that means you'll need to experiment to see what keeps words flowing for you. But the overview below should help you decide how you want to start.

Winging It

This approach is also called pantsing it, as in flying by the seat of your pants. Personally, I like the term discovery writer, which I heard first from author Joanna Penn. You discover your plot, and perhaps all your story elements, as you write.

On first glance, it's the easiest way to start a novel and feels like the most fun because all you do is dive in and write. No need to know where the story going, and you're open to all sorts of twists and turns along the way. As a storyteller, it's the most similar to sitting around a camp fire and making up a ghost story on the fly.

The pros of discovery writing include, for many writers, more excitement and a greater feeling of freedom and creativity. It's like a live wire act. Also, some writers prefer winging it because they feel if they know what's coming, the readers will too, which undercuts the dramatic tension.

Also, you may feel tense or hemmed in with all or part of your story planned in advance.

Cons include a lot of writing to figure out where you're going, which can lead to discarding large parts of your novel or many additional hours revising or both. (I learned this from personal experience with one of my early novels.) Also, writing without a plot may leave you staring more often at a blank screen, which can lead to anxiety and feeling stuck.

Finally, if you're someone who feels best with routines or likes to plan other parts of your life, writing by the seat of your pants may leave you feeling generally uneasy and make the writing process less fun.

That last point is probably the biggest reason I don't, for the most part, like discovery writing. I relax much more when I have some sense of what's next, whether that's in life or writing, while understanding that I need to be flexible because nothing's set in stone.

The Major Points And Turns

The way I write novels now is to think through and write out major points in advance. Specifically, I figure out at least these plot points:

- Opening Conflict (to draw the reader into the characters' world)
- Story Spark (also known as an Inciting Incident – the event that sets the main plot in motion)
- The One-Quarter Twist (the first major plot turn that takes the story in a new direction, usually it comes about 25% through the book)
- The Midpoint (more on this in Chapter 19)
- The Three-Quarter Turn (last major plot turn, spins the story again, usually happens about 75% through)
- The Climax (final conflict between protagonist and antagonist that reaches resolution)
- Falling Action (resolves subplots, ties up loose ends)

To figure these out I do a lot of rambling on paper or in a Word document. (If you want to know more about this structure, you can download free Story Structure worksheets at WritingAsASecond-Career.com/Story, or buy one of my books on writing, which are listed in the last chapter. I also write notes about what happens in between the points. Sometimes I scribble about subplots. And for my mysteries, I type notes in a chart about four or five suspects with basic information about them.

The first half of my main plot and the Climax usually track what I planned pretty well, though all of it is subject to change as I write. The second half usually changes more. New or different subplots arise as I write, and characters morph, appear, and disappear. Because I'm open to new directions, I don't feel hemmed in or stifled by the planning process.

As you've probably guessed, it takes time to sort through these major points before writing. That's why this approach doesn't necessarily save time over discovery writing. For me, though, it feels like it takes less time because once I do start writing the novel, I first draft quickly. And I rarely feel stuck.

A Detailed Outline

Finally, you can prepare a detailed outline. Some writers create bullet point lists or virtual or paper index cards with short descriptions of each scene. A fantasy author I heard speak at a conference said he creates 80-page outlines for 350-page novels. In essence, they are first drafts that need dialogue, description, and characterization added. Working from the long outline, he dictates his first draft into his computer.

I tried my own version of this once, writing out a page-long description for each scene in a spiral notebook. Later, at my computer, I wrote the novel straight through based on those pages. This approach made good use of my time and work situation, as I was doing temp office work on and off. On lunch breaks or when no one had any work for me, I scribbled my scenes. Then during the weeks I took off from work I wrote the novel.

I was happy with the result, but I didn't enjoy the writing very much. Also, looking back, I feel like it kept me from exploring what could have been some more interesting character developments and plot turns.

But many writers prefer detailed outlines. They explore plot turns and delve into character growth, subplots, and settings in advance. Then once they start to first draft, they know at each step of the way what happens next. This approach also usually shortens the rewriting that's needed.

What's Best For You?

Finding the approach that works for you can have a huge impact on how much you enjoy writing and how seldom you feel blocked. It both keeps the words flowing and helps you identify what's going on if you are struggling.

The only way to know what works best for you, though, is to try different ways. See what you enjoy and what makes it easiest for you to write. It's also worth experimenting again later in your career. What works best at one point may not be ideal at another.

Now let's get to the writing itself. Specifically, writing what I think of as your zero draft.

Questions

- Have you tried outlining a novel before?
- What was the result?
- Do you know any of the major plot turns for your novel?
- Which of the approaches described in this chapter do you want to try?

_____

_____

_____

_____

_____

_____

_____

_____

_____

_____

_____

_____

_____

_____

_____

_____

_____

_____

9

WRITING FAST AND FUN WITH THE ZERO DRAFT

A couple years ago I attended a talk by author Rachael Herron, and she used a term I hadn't heard before: the zero draft. When she explained it, I realized she was describing the initial very rough draft that I never show anyone.

My zero drafts:

- ramble
- include storylines that trail off to nowhere and others that start mid-stream
- include incorrect character names and characters who disappear
- are filled with errors.

And that's the good parts.

I'm certain that's why, other than when I skipped the rough outline phase I mentioned in Chapter 8, I've never felt blocked during that draft of any novel. If you know mostly where you're going, you can write the zero draft on the fly. If you're a discovery writer, you can still do that, as you're essentially figuring out where you're going as you write. Your zero draft may include more rambles and turns and twists to revise later than if you started with an outline, but you'll still write quickly.

That's because giving yourself the green light on Day One to write a draft that includes the issues discussed above shuts off that editor side of your brain. You know many parts of the draft will be bad and possibly unreadable. And you also know you won't show it to anyone. Ever.

So there's no reason to go back and fix anything as you write. And there's no reason not to keep writing all the way to the end.

What To Include In Your Zero Draft

Your aim with the zero draft is to write a beginning, middle, and end. In other words, a complete story, however you get there. My early drafts tend to be more detailed in the first two-thirds where I'm more sure where I'm going, and a bit thinner on anything other than plot in the last third where I'm more apt to depart from my rough outline.

That's okay. Later I'll rearrange and expand.

You can explore characters in your zero draft, rambling into backstory or side scenes if it helps you. Some writers play with different endings or themes. The key is to get an entire story on paper (or screen) so you can look at it as a whole later.

And remember, it doesn't need to be a perfect story or a final version of the plot or subplots.

When I was writing the zero draft of my second supernatural thriller, *The Unbelievers*, I realized that I rarely covered how my protagonist felt about her baby (a girl with her own destiny and powers) or where the baby was exactly. My protagonist, Tara, was deeply devoted to her daughter, loved her fiercely, and had vowed to protect her. But in most scenes the baby didn't matter to the plot.

I made a note to address this issue in rewrites and ignored it during the zero draft. When the novel when was nearly done I specifically looked at each scene and asked myself where the baby was and what Tara felt about her, then wove that in. Ironically, I got reader feedback that they found Tara's feelings authentic and moving, and were amazed how I'd included that without slowing the action-adventure type pace of the novel.

What Not To Worry About In Your Zero Draft

It's easier to write a zero draft than a first draft because there are a host of things that usually slow the writing process that you can ignore, including continuity.

For example, if you decide to change a character's backstory or the plot in the middle of the book, don't go back and revise. Instead, write yourself a note, ideally in your document when you decided to change course. Then go on ahead as if you already made the earlier changes. During my zero draft, I changed a plot development relating to the antagonist, Cyril, in my first *Awakening* thriller. When I made that change, I didn't go back and edit the earlier scenes. Instead, I typed this into my document and went right on: *[change so Cyril stalks Tara before she meets him]*.

This approach saves you from going back and revising the early chapters, or perhaps the first half, of your novel each time you have a new idea. This will save you a lot of time if you reach the end and realize you don't need that character after all, or you're dropping that sub-plot that seemed so brilliant when you were halfway through. Though I kept the Cyril change, there were other plot developments I noted that by the end of my zero draft I discovered I didn't want to do.

Also, knowing you've done this leaves most writers feeling freer to write on in the face of uncertainty about the storyline. If you're not sure what direction to go, tell yourself it's just the zero draft, so you can always veer another way. Then choose an option and move on.

Characters can also morph and change significantly during your zero draft or when you make revisions. To love your story, your reader needs to be engaged with your characters. But the zero draft isn't the time to worry about that. If I know a character well and the words flow about that person, that character is often the most three-dimensional in the entire draft.

But sometimes I know only that a character needs to fill a

certain role – sidekick to the antagonist, alternate suspect in a mystery, the protagonist's supportive boss or mentor – and I haven't worked out who that person is. Then I simply write that character doing whatever it is I need the character to do and leave it to later drafts to create a believable person with strong motivations.

Some characters don't even get names.

In the zero draft of *The Charming Man*, Book 2 in my Q.C. Davis mystery series, I've got characters "named" Neighbor1 and Neighbor2. Despite that I figured out and filled in the second neighbor only on later drafts, and he says about ten lines total, he became a side character that many readers commented on and enjoyed. (Something you never would have guessed from the zero draft.)

Also don't worry if you don't feel like the writing's flowing or the pace of the story will be fast enough. I've written passages that struck me as clunky and slow-moving that ultimately turned out to be some of the best writing I'd ever done with a few tweaks. Other times I sped through pages and pages on what felt like a runner's high (guessing on that as I hate running and never get a runner's high) only to later cut two-thirds of what I wrote.

Consciously Let Go Of Perfectionism

If you find yourself revising your scenes multiple times before writing on, you're likely trying too hard to make it good, great, or perfect. This can be especially hard if you work in another profession or pursue another interest where you need to be detail focused and get everything just right before you go to the next task.

There are a very small percentage of writers who labor over every line or paragraph before moving on, and when the first draft is finished it's pretty close to final. But for most of us, especially early in our careers, getting a novel finished means letting go of perfect at the early stages so you can get to the end.

Remember, a first draft is a thing of beauty not because it's perfect, but because it's done. So the biggest key to getting beyond your initial scenes or chapters – no matter how much time you have or don't – is being willing to write something bad, then to move on and write the next part of the book and the next and the next.

At the end you can revisit, rewrite, and polish all you want.

Marketing Can Wait

How you'll market your novel also can wait for later, especially if this is your first book. That's because thinking about marketing engages the editor part of your brain. It raises a whole separate set of concerns, and will cause you to start asking questions about whether the genre you're writing will be popular by the time you finish, or whether anyone but you will love your characters.

None of those fears, which I'll talk about more in Part 3, will help you finish your novel. They're more likely to slow you down or bring you to a halt.

If you thought about marketing while choosing an idea, trust your judgment and remind yourself that now it's writing time. If you didn't, there's time to consider whether or how you'll share you work with the world later.

Finally, as I noted in the last chapter, skip line editing in the zero draft. Just write. It's the best and quickest way to get your novel on paper.

Now that we've talked about getting ideas and writing that early draft, let's talk about where you'll write it, which can affect how easily and quickly your words flow.

Questions

- **Do you feel comfortable writing a zero draft?**
- **If not, what could you do to convince yourself that it's okay?**
- **What parts of the draft are you most apt to want to revise or get stuck in?**
- **How will you address them?**

10

WHERE YOU WRITE CAN HELP YOU STAY UNSTUCK

In the next chapter I'll talk about carving out time to write. But knowing in advance where you'll write can also help ensure you keep writing on. If you're already racing through your draft, you might be able to write almost anywhere. But if you're feeling stuck, a personal writing space can help you relax, trigger your urge to write, and spark ideas.

Location, Location, Location

The place where you'll more enjoy writing depends on many factors. Here are key ones to think about:

- what else you do there
- who else is there
- how you feel there
- what makes it easier

What Else You Do

If you are someone who feels the need to do laundry if it's in front of you, load the dishwasher as soon as you finish eating, or sweep the floor after every meal, first, come to my house. I will write while you do those things.

Second, working at home might pose challenges for you whether or not you have space for it.

It's all too easy to decide to throw in a load of laundry before you start writing. It seems like it won't take much time. But in about half an hour, you'll need to switch it to the dryer. In another hour, you'll need to take it out and fold it. Now if you were lucky enough to set aside two hours to write, you've spent about twenty minutes of it on laundry. In short, if you're having trouble writing chores at home make it far too easy to walk away from your laptop or notebook.

Be honest with yourself. If you spend 15-20% or more of your writing time on other things at home, try writing somewhere else.

A public space can be a good choice. Why?

Because the barista at Starbucks won't ask you to clean the cappuccino machine, and the librarian will not expect you to reshelve books. Put your phone on silent, leave books, ear buds, and children (appropriately supervised, of course!) at home, and don't connect to the Internet. There will be nothing for you to do but write.

If you have an office or other isolated space at another job, you may want to try writing there. A few recommendations if you do:

- Set aside a spot where you put your notes on your writing project and anything else that relates to writing. That way you won't waste time digging it out or organizing it.
- Unless it's impossible to do for your job, turn off email notifications, forward your phone to voicemail, and block off the time on your calendar. (If the only way you can find time to write is to be available for emails or telephone calls, try ignoring them for 15 or 20 minutes at a time, then checking in. Odds are, you can be away for that amount of time, and if there's no emergency, proceed for another 15 or 20 minutes.)
- Even if you're paid for results or tasks, not by the hour,

it's probably best not to tell people at work that you are writing a novel while you're there. They will view you as "not working" and feel free to interrupt you to chat. They also may start to imagine you're not as attentive as you should be even if you are.

If work tasks distract you the way chores at home do, though, a public space like a coffee shop or library is likely the better choice. Or if you're lucky enough to have a friend with a quiet space you can use in their home or their workplace, and that friend will leave you alone, that might be the best option of all.

Who Else Is There

If you live with other people or pets, give some thought to how that affects your writing. That's because asking others to carve out writing space and time for you almost never works. You need to make it a priority before anyone else will. This is why I simply don't answer email or phone calls when I'm writing unless I have a break scheduled already. If I answer and say, "I only have a moment, I'm writing," the person on the other end nearly always keeps talking. And why not? I answered the phone.

Also, if you have children, a significant other, or pets, it may feel wrong to ignore them no matter how much you want to write.

For those reasons, you may find you write more easily in one of the non-home places I talked about above.

How You Feel

Whatever it looks like and however it fits with the rest of your life, the space where you write needs to be somewhere you feel good. This is especially so if you have another demanding career or other responsibilities.

Choose a space or spaces, however large or small, where you can relax and focus. You may need to try out several places, both public and private. That may include experimenting with things like ways to physically screen off a corner in a room to figuring out what time you need to arrive in a public space to get the most isolated spot.

Physical comfort also is key. If writing is uncomfortable or hurts your body, you won't want to do it. Make sure your keyboard, chair, and monitor or screen heights don't hurt your body. This may mean skipping the counter stool with a window view in favor of a chair with a back at the coffee shop. Or getting an adjustable desk or chair at home.

Temperature may also matter for you. Personally, I need to be physically warm. If I'm shivering, I find it hard to think. On those occasions when I write in a public space in the winter, I make sure to sit far from the door where icy wind blows in each time someone enters. And if a coffee shop is too cold, I abandon it until summer comes.

The noise level matters too. If you need quiet and can't find it, noise-cancelling headphones, if in your budget, can be a lifesaver. (Otherwise try the library.) On the other hand, if background noise is useful and you can't get to café, try playing nature sounds on your computer (or a CD if you, like me, still have old tech) or coffee-house sounds.

A Moment's Motivation

Give some thought as well to what motivates you to get to your keyboard in the moment. If getting out of the house appeals to you, you're more likely to write if you make that your plan. But if it's easier to simply roll out of bed and sit at your writing desk, do that.

In that sense, writing is a lot like exercise. You may be more apt to do it if you buy a health club membership, but for me, needing to walk or drive to a gym and change clothes before I exercise means I'll never get there. But I roll out my yoga mat every morning at home. Likewise, I write the most when I have a nice writing space at home, despite occasionally liking to write elsewhere.

Change It Up

Whatever space you choose to write in, every once in a while try something different. For one thing, you may not yet know where you do your best work or feel happiest writing. Also, as your life changes, where you prefer to write will change as well.

All right, let's talk about when you write.

~

Questions

- What are your options for writing spaces?
- Which ones have worked best for you in the past?
- Is there anything you can change in your preferred writing spot to make writing easier and more fun?

_____
_____
_____
_____
_____
_____
_____
_____
_____
_____
_____
_____
_____
_____
_____
_____
_____

11

YOUR WRITING TIME

When you write and how you use that time also affects how easy or challenging it will be to get your novel started.

Nobody has extra hours in the day or the week, and nobody starts out getting paid to devote hours to writing a novel. That means it's up to you to find the time to write and to make the most of it. This chapter includes tips on doing both.

Let's start, though, with your non-writing life.

The Big Picture

Choices you make in the non-writing parts of your life can make it simpler or more challenging to find time to write. So when you can, think about how other life decisions will affect your writing. Writing isn't the only factor, of course, especially for major choices. If you've always wanted children, for instance, the fact that having them will almost certainly mean less time to write (I'm assuming you want to spend some time with them, right?) likely won't change your plans. But writing might affect whether you live far or near to a day job, what type of other work you do, and whether you choose to commute by car or train.

When I hunted for job right out of college, for example, I always asked how much overtime was expected. I didn't say it, but I was looking for, and found, a job where I usually got to go home at five p.m. so that I could write in the evenings. And when I became a lawyer, I understood that I was choosing to focus on that profession for the foreseeable future, with my writing taking second place to my obligations to my clients.

Not everyone has the luxury of arranging parts of their lives around writing. There were many times when I didn't have it and needed to take whatever job I could get wherever it was. But if you do have options, give some thought to how to make it easier to write. That way you won't be as likely to feel you're shirking other responsibilities when you write, which can lead to feeling guilty and blocked.

Your Best Writing Time

Giving some thought to when during your day or week you're most productive can help you form a writing habit and start writing pages.

Most of us feel sharper at certain times of the day and more creative during others. If you're a morning person, you may want to reserve some of that time for your novel even if it means waking earlier each day. If you're a night owl, though, you may be more creative, and your words may flow more easily, late at night.

How much time you have in one sitting matters too. I am most productive on a first draft or my first rewrite, and I feel the best, when I can set aside large chunks of time to work on a single project. I take periodic breaks, but I love to immerse myself in the fictional world and focus on it to the exclusion of everything else. That helps me keep track of plot twists and character development, which I find harder if I'm working in half-hour bursts.

Because of that, if I'm able to work it out with the rest of my schedule, I'd rather write for 2 or 3 hours at a stretch one day a week than half an hour a day for 5 days.

Other people, though, like to shift from task to task and feel antsy or frustrated when they spend hours on one project.

Your best writing time may also be concentrated in a week that you take off from work. As a lawyer, I usually took what I thought of as writing vacations. When I was able to take five days off in a row, I stayed home and wrote 5-6 hours a day. (I had to have a little free time in there!).

If you can figure out your best time to write and make that work at least some of the time, it'll make writing your novel more fun. And it'll go faster. If you can't arrange the rest of your life around your writing, though, there are still ways to keep the words flowing in whatever time you do have. I'll talk about those in Part 2.

Where Do You Find The Time

Let's say you want to add a half hour of writing time a day to your schedule. Before you figure out when it will be, the more important question is what it will replace.

For example, if you say, "I'm going to get up a half hour earlier each morning and write before work," you're either deciding to sleep an hour less at night, or to go to bed an hour earlier each night, which means skipping something else. Whether that thing is reading to your kids at night, watching the news or TV before you go to sleep, getting in an hour of work for your day job, or something else, somewhere, somehow, that half hour comes from somewhere.

If you don't make a choice about what it will be, it's far more likely you won't head for your keyboard during that 30 minutes. Or if you do, you'll feel constantly behind or worried you should be doing some other task, resulting in freezing as you stare at the screen or getting, at best, a sentence or two written.

Either way, you may experience this as being stuck or blocked because it feels like you just can't get yourself to write.

So instead, for a week or two note what you do with each hour of your time. Then, being both creative and realistic, decide what activity or activities you'll skip so that you can write. Pay special attention to what you dislike doing. It's a lot easier to swap in writing for something you'd rather not do anyway.

Being creative means looking at various ways to cut out on an activity. For instance, if you can afford it, and you currently spend two hours a week cleaning your house and don't enjoy it, pay someone else to do that while you write. Or if you spend half an hour a night watching the news, but the news stresses you out, ask a well-informed friend to tell you if there's anything you really need to know, turn off the news, and write for that half hour.

Realism also matters. If paying someone to clean your house will strain your budget to the extreme, you won't be able to relax and write even if you find a way to manage the expense. Or if you're like me and cutting back on sleep leaves you too disoriented to focus or makes you sick, staying up an hour later or getting up an hour earlier every day will result in less useful writing time (and might injure your health).

You may find there are activities you're simply not willing to cut even if you think you are. Let's say you plan to skip the 30 minutes at night when you read a book before going to sleep. That might seem reasonable, but if it turns out you're unable to sleep or you keep skipping writing and reading anyway, probably your mind or body needs that wind down time.

But remember, you don't necessarily need to stop doing something entirely. You can instead look for ways to spend less time on it. One businesswoman I know said she spent less time on laundry each week by no longer folding sheets (especially the fitted ones). She just bunches them up and puts them in a drawer. By itself I can't imagine that saves a huge amount of time. But combined with 5 or 6 other time savers it can add up to an extra hour or two a week.

This can apply to recreation, too. For instance, if you play basketball every week with a friend and that's the only free time you could switch to writing, maybe play every other week rather than quitting entirely.

Scheduling And Spare Change

Whatever you decide to cut, you'll be more apt to write if you plan for writing time the same way you set other appointments in your calendar. Take out your calendar (or scheduling app) at the same time each weekend and book your writing appointments with yourself for the following week.

Then as you go through your week, get in front of your keyboard or notebook during the time you set aside. If you're not sure what to write, write about that. It will reinforce your habit of writing.

If your schedule varies widely from day to day, as mine did when I ran my own law firm, I still suggest putting in a few blocks of time a week in advance. Your goal can be to write at least 2 or 3 times out of the 4 or 5 scheduled appointments. If you write during all of them, hooray. If not, you'll get in more writing than if you didn't schedule it.

Or you can try what one of my favorite writing instructors, Raymond Obstfeld, called the spare change method. You set a goal of a number of pages per month (or several months). Then, rather than writing X amount per day or week, you throw whatever you can into the writing equivalent of the spare change jar, keeping track of how many words you wrote until you hit that goal.

I used the spare change method during the years I practiced law full time because my schedule was never predicable. One week I might write 12 pages, the next week 4, and the next none at all. But at the end of the month, I'd written 20 or 30 pages.

If you opt for that method, each week you might write in your calendar: *Write 2,000 words this week.* Or at the beginning of the month: *Write 10,000 words this month.* If you average out to more or less than that over time, you can adjust the goal.

On the other hand, if your life is fairly predictable, you can schedule a month in advance or simply set a recurring time in your calendar for the whole year.

Why all this emphasis on scheduling in a book about writer's block? The more decisions you need to make in the moment, the more likely it is you'll opt for something else. Make it easy and decide once in advance.

Finally, keep in mind that if you have a cyclical work life or a chronic physical or mental condition that affects when you are well enough to write, your schedule or goal will need to be more flexible. You might focus on hours per 3-month or 6-month period rather than per week.

That's okay. Even if you don't write as much as you hoped, you'll write something.

Prompt Your Unconscious

As I talked about earlier, much of the creative process takes place behind the scenes in your unconscious mind. While you're busy doing something else, your unconscious can come up with story ideas and scenes and flesh out characters. Which is terrific because it means that when you do find those few minutes or, if you're lucky, hours, you'll be able to write easily and quickly.

The activities in the chapters on ideas are designed to stimulate this unconscious process. You can also direct your unconscious mind more deliberately. Over the years, I often asked myself questions as I got into bed at night or before heading to my law office in the morning. As an example, when I was working a lot of hours and writing the first book in my *Awakening* series, I asked: *Where is the most unnerving place for Tara to be confronted by a stranger who claims to know the meaning of her pregnancy?*

If I ask a question like that every so often, then put it out of my mind, eventually a scene or idea pops into my head. In that example, the scene takes place just before midnight in a deserted Laundromat where Tara works. The stranger enters as she's closing for the night.

Before you go to sleep tonight, try asking yourself a question about a character or story. If you're lucky, it will prompt a dream you'll remember that touches on the question. I personally am rarely that lucky. But I almost always find new ideas drifting into my mind the following day.

Use Your Downtime

Downtime can also be a great way to help yourself write once you do get to your keyboard. While my law practice was extremely busy, I still had downtime. While you don't see it on TV shows about lawyers, almost all of us spend time waiting. Sometimes I'm sitting in a courtroom as long as 40 or 50 minutes waiting to give the judge a status report about a case. I've also spent many flight-delayed hours at airport gates when traveling to visit clients or take depositions.

That's why I carry a legal pad in my shoulder bag or briefcase and pull it out if I have more than five minutes. (You can also use the note function on your phone for this, but judges frown on lawyers appearing to be emailing or playing on their phones while in the courtroom, so I write on paper.)

I particularly like scribbling about characters, because if I'm cut off in the middle it doesn't matter. In fact, my unconscious will probably keep going with the train of thought. Now and then I write snippets of dialogue or openings for scenes. While the legal pad pages rarely make their way to my writing desk, and the exact words almost never get typed into a manuscript, my thoughts flow more freely when I do have time. It's a big part of why, when my practice was at its busiest, I was always able to turn out pages as soon as I sat down to write fiction.

Even if your job doesn't include waiting time, you still run into it in real life.

If you're stuck waiting in line at a store or are outside your child's school at the end of the day, you can ask yourself questions about your characters or your plot. You can observe the people around you. Notice their chins, their noses, how they carry themselves, their expressions. Think about how you'd describe them in writing. This can be especially helpful if your physical descriptions of characters tend to get repetitive or rely too much on describing eye color, hair color, and height.

You can also do these types of exercises, mentally or in writing, when you feel too worn out to write scenes. If you just got home from work or finally put your two-year-old down for a nap, grab a paper and pen or your phone and scribble, type, or talk out a character or story question and answer. Do this often enough and by the time you get to your keyboard you'll be in great shape to write the first scene or the next one.

I hope by now you have a pretty good idea how to get ideas and write your early pages. Or you've already done both. If so, congratulate yourself! Many people say they want to write a novel. Many of them take a class or buy a book about how to do it. But a much smaller number take the first step and start writing.

All the same, the beginning is just, well, the beginning. Now you need to write on through the middle and to the end. That middle can be especially challenging. Usually the excitement of the early stages wears off a bit, and you're too far from the end to feel the thrill that comes with finishing. It can still be fun, though, and exciting. Especially if you understand what motivates you the most and learn some tricks for keeping the moment going. Which is what we'll talk about in Part 2.

Questions

- **What tasks might you be able to stop doing or do more efficiently so you can find time to write?**
- **When are you most likely to have downtime?**
- **Do you use a calendar, app, or program to manage your weekly schedule?**
- **During what part of the day do you feel the most focused?**
- **The most imaginative?**

_____

_____

_____

_____

_____

_____

_____

_____

PART II

KEEP THE BALL ROLLING

12

MOTIVATING YOURSELF TO WRITE

Last winter I talked with a friend who'd fallen on the ice for the second time that year. She confided that she has always had trouble with balance, and she worries because as she ages the potential for serious injury increases. I asked if her doctor suggested anything to improve her balance and prevent falling. She said oh, yes, she has ten minutes of balance exercises to do each day.

But she never does them.

Like my friend, most of us have things that we could do regularly that would make us happier and healthier and help us reach our goals. We know what they are, yet often it's hard to follow through.

That's particularly so when we're talking about something where we need to work at it right now but won't see the final results for a long time. Like writing and finishing a novel.

What Motivates You

Many writers find the initial excitement about writing a novel carries them through the first quarter or third of a book, but then they start to slow down. Sometimes you write up to your first major plot turn and don't know where to go next, which I'll talk about later on in this section. Other times you need to strengthen your overall commitment or your regular writing habits, which I'll also cover.

But sometimes it's an issue of what most motivates you, not just in writing but in all of life, and how best to tap into that.

In *The Four Tendencies: The Indispensable Personality Profiles That Reveal How to Make Your Life Better (and Other People's Lives Better, Too)*, author Gretchen Rubin writes about research showing people tend to feel most motivated to meet goals for one of four reasons. While it's not a book about writing, and I'm inclined to be a bit wary of categorizing people's psyches, I do find the book lays out a useful framework for understanding what might make a writer more or less likely to finish a novel.

These tendencies help explain, for example, why using a word count chart helps me finish a first draft on time, causes another writer to say, "Why would I ever do that?" and leaves yet another less likely to write at all.

For that reason, after some suggestions on getting leverage on yourself to stay motivated, I'll share how I see those four tendencies Rubin talks about applying to novel writing. Any errors in describing her theories are mine. (If you'd like to see her original work, you can read her book *The Four Tendencies: The Indispensable Personality Profiles That Reveal How to Make Your Life Better (and Other People's Lives Better, Too)*.

Getting Leverage On Yourself

You probably first heard of leverage in connection with moving physical objects. It literally means exerting force by means of a lever. It also means to support or strengthen. When it comes to writing a novel, to get leverage on yourself means to use a consequence (internal or external) or outside force to exert more pressure on yourself.

A Tale Of Two Friends

A few years ago I attended a business for authors conference. Author and organizer Dean Wesley Smith talked about when he was a college student taking a writing class.

He and his friend both wanted to write a story every week and submit it to a magazine. To help meet their goal, they agreed to meet for dinner once a week. Whoever had failed to complete a new story and mail it (this was back when you had to actually print and mail your manuscripts) would buy dinner.

As both were students and neither had much money, the fear of needing to pay for dinner got both of them to finish and submit stories weekly. The agreement between these two friends is a great example of using leverage and accountability to meet writing goals.

Accountability

Dictionaries define accountability as an obligation or the willingness to accept responsibility for one's own actions. That's why we say corporations are accountable to shareholders.

On a personal level, by telling someone you trust your goals and setting a schedule for reporting your progress (or lack of it) you become accountable to that person. It's much harder to skip doing something if you not only must admit it to yourself but to someone else.

Dean Wesley Smith's story includes accountability. In addition to the cost of a meal, he'd need to admit to his friend that he'd failed to do something he'd said he would or, on the flipside, he'd get to enjoy reporting that he'd accomplished his weekly goal.

Getting The Leverage To Finish Your Novel

Here are some ways to create leverage and accountability to help you finish your novel, a few of which come from my book *The One-Year Novelist: A Week-By-Week Guide To Writing Your Novel In One Year*:

- Tell three people that you will finish your novel by a specific date that you choose. Ask each one if you can check in (via email, text, or some other type of message) every week to share an update on your progress. If you're someone motivated by obligations to other people, ask those people to contact you and ask what's going on if you don't update them. You can also ask them to inquire further if you aren't getting many pages written. But if you're someone motivated by internal goals, simply reporting without getting a response will help you keep writing until the end.

- If one or more of those people is willing and you want more outside pressure, have a phone conversation where the person asks how you're doing.

Caveat: I don't suggest relying on posting on social media. While it's true that many people may see your goal and your periodic progress posts, there's no guarantee that the same people will see them each time. Having to tell specific people who will follow your progress creates a lot more pressure and accountability.

- If you haven't already done so, write in detail about why you're excited about writing your novel, how you'll feel if you finish it, and how you'll feel if you don't. Look at these written feelings to spur you on as you write or when you're tempted not to write.
- If you want to add accountability, share what you wrote with a trusted friend and ask that person to remind you of what you said from time to time.

Positive consequences can also work as leverage. Happily, your imagination can help with this.

- Close your eyes and imagine the moment you finish your novel. If you like to type The End, see those words on the screen. If, like me, you like to print out your manuscript to review, envision the printer shooting out the pages. Get in touch with the sense of accomplishment you'll feel.
- Plan a reward for when you finish your novel. It could be a weekend away, a longer vacation, or something as simple as a fancy latte at Starbucks. Whatever it is,

though, it's something you vow you won't do until you finish your novel.

If you've got a lot of words to write before you get to the end, you can set up a couple rewards in between.

Now let's talk about those tendencies I mentioned. Where you fall among them can affect what type of leverage works best for you.

Loves Rules, Charts, And Deadlines - The Upholder

If you fit what Rubin calls the Upholder tendency you almost always meet your own goals as well as other people's expectations. It's probably easy for you to form habits, including a writing habit. You typically get the things done that you want to do whether or not anyone else pushes you to do them.

One downside, which I've experienced, is you may be so driven that you meet everyone's expectations plus your own that you forget to leave time to relax. That can be particularly challenging for your novel writing because, as I talked about earlier, relaxing plays such an important part in creativity.

You'll be most likely to stay focused on your novel if you set a clear goal of finishing it, as well as interim goals. To Do lists, charts, and tracking how much you write are probably great motivators. (I love to check off boxes!)

It's also important to take time regularly to reassess your goals – and your obligations to others – to be sure they still make sense. If you set a goal of writing three romance novels, for example, but after you finish the first one you realize you don't like writing romance, it's okay to reconsider the goal. You may still go ahead with it, but you'll know why you're doing it and that you feel it's worth it rather than plowing full steam ahead and yet feeling frustrated because you don't see the point of it or would rather be writing something else.

Meeting Other People's Demands - The Obligor

According to Rubin, if the Obligor is your tendency, you do everything you promised anyone else you would do. Friends, family, and coworkers all know they can rely on you. But you may find it hard to get done what you want to do, including making progress on your novel, if no one else asks or requires you to do it.

For example, if you and a friend agree to go to the gym at seven a.m. each day, you'll be there to meet your friend even if you have to drag yourself out of bed. But if you decide on a solo early morning exercise plan, you may very well skip it after the first day. And then feel upset about what you see as a lack of follow through.

Writers who are obligors often find it easiest to meet their writing goals where there is outside accountability. So rather than giving yourself a hard time if you don't finish that writing project on your To Do list, enlist other people to help you stay on track.

One way is to take a class that includes deadlines for turning in scenes or chapters. If you have trouble finding a class that focuses on novels, though, you can look for writing workshops where participants exchange or read pages. The plus of such a workshop is that if you don't write, other group members will ask you why not.

The minus is you'll likely spend significant time reading other writers' work and may end in skimping on your own. That's one reason you may be better off with a more personal and tailored method of accountability.

Another example is to find a writing buddy and meet for dinner periodically, as Dean Wesley Smith did. But add a twist if you're an Obligor. If you don't get your pages written, your friend will have to buy you dinner and vice versa. That's because as an Obligor, you're probably more motivated if your lack of follow through inconveniences your friend, not you. You don't want your friend to have to spend more money because you didn't write your pages, right?

Obviously, make sure your friend is an Obligor, too, and is okay with being on the hook if you don't come through. If that's not in the budget, you could try buying one another a cup of coffee instead, and put a limit on it, such as if either of you has to buy three times in a row, the arrangement is off. Because you'll want your friend to keep getting the benefit of your deal, you're likely to write your pages.

These types of options, or others that you think of along the same lines, can make it much easier to write on and on through the middle of your novel.

Why Should I Write Today? - The Questioner

Questioners want to know why they should do things. If you lean this way, you're the most motivated to do something when all your questions about it are answered and you feel satisfied the reasons for doing it are solid. This is true whether it's a personal goal or one someone else expects you to take on.

On the upside, once you're convinced you follow through. Also, you're unlikely to take on too many projects without thinking it through. But you might spend too much time on thinking about what's the best place to write, which computer is the best choice, or where each scene should be set, which can hinder getting through the middle and to the end of your novel.

If you're a Questioner, spend some time writing out exactly why you want to write a novel and why this particular novel. You may also need to spend more time than other writers do on finding a good writing space and making sure you figure out how to fit writing into your schedule without undermining your relationships or other responsibilities. Doing so will help you keep writing through that middle part of the book.

Pay attention, though, to when you keep going around and around the same questions. If that's happening, try writing out your answers, then setting a specific date to revisit them (say, every five or six chapters or at the end of each month). Doing that can help you stay in touch with your reasons for writing a novel and answer any new questions that may be nagging at you and sapping your motivation.

No One Tells Me What To Do - The Rebel

If you have Rebel tendencies, you may resist all expectations – your own and anyone else's. If someone tells you to do something, you immediately don't want to do it. At the same time, you might jump right in if someone tells you that you can't do something. For example, if an English teacher friend says you'll never make it as a writer, you might work hard and take great delight in proving that person wrong.

The great part of leaning toward the Rebel side is you're unlikely to be defined by others' expectations. On the downside, you may find it hard to meet any goal, including one you choose yourself, or to set a goal at all, as it feels confining.

If you have Rebel tendencies, you are more likely to be drawn toward the creativity, free thinking, and romance of novel writing and to feel stifled by planning either your plot or your writing time.

That's okay. If a set schedule makes your blood run cold or an outline makes writing feel too much like work, you don't need either. Perhaps instead you can see writing as your private time, set aside for just you and no one else.

Also, while most writers get more done if they focus on writing their novel straight through from start to finish, you may need the freedom to write in any order. Try writing the scenes that interest you most in the moment and weave them together into an order later. You also may want to have various projects in the works so you can always choose the one that appeals to you rather than feeling like you're sitting down to do your homework.

No Matter What Motivates You...

Regardless of your tendency or whether you fit any of these categories, as with everything in this book experiment to see what works for you. Then experiment again down the road. Charts and schedules may be wonderful for keeping you on task at one time in your life. But during another you may need the freedom of the Rebel. The key isn't finding one right approach for all time. It's finding what makes writing easiest right now.

In Chapters 14-18, I'll talk about some practical nuts-and-bolts ways you can make it easier to write. But first, let's talk more specifically about why you want to write a novel in the first place.

Question

- Did you identify with any of the four tendencies?
- Which one?
- Does that change any of your plans for writing?

13

YOUR WHY, WHAT YOU LOVE, AND YOUR MISSION

If you've wanted to write a novel forever and you've gotten a good start, it may seem odd to pause and ask yourself why. But staying in touch with why you write will carry you through those moments, and every novelist has them, when the last thing you feel like doing is finishing that scene, figuring out that plot question, or cutting out that character and trying a different one. It can also help you become energized again in moments when you start stalling out or feel tired of trying.

Your Mission

One way to get at why you're writing a novel is to craft a mission statement for it (or for a series of novels if that's what you're planning).

In the business world, a mission statement is a summary, or sometimes a tag line, about the purpose and values of an organization or person. Corporations and non-profits often use them to guide their growth or focus the people who work for them.

I'll talk in a moment about how the idea applies to fiction. But first, a few words on why I didn't suggest writing one before you began your novel.

The When Of The Why

I waited until now to talk about mission statements for a number of reasons.

First, for some writers, including me, at the early stages it can make novel writing feel weightier, which in turn makes it harder to start writing. I feel pretty free to dive in, with or without an outline or plan, if my goal is to write an entertaining story that along the way conveys something about life.

But if I tell myself I want to write a novel that will change the world, well, yikes. That sounds like it requires a lot of thought, planning, hubris, focus, high-level concepts....plus a very important person to do it.

Also, readers generally want a good story first. If you're too focused on getting a message out there you risk writing something more like an essay or persuasive speech than a novel.

In addition, as with anything else, at some point you only learn to write a novel by doing it. Adding another layer of preparing can tempt you to delay writing, especially if you're feeling a little apprehensive or already struggle to get words on the page.

Finally, often you need to write a significant amount of your novel before you have a sense of why it means so much to you. As with plotting your story or creating your characters, I believe much of what motivates us to write is unconscious. Trying to sort it out ahead of time might only lead to frustration.

But as you delve into the writing, you'll get more and more in touch with why it matters to you. And that can keep you motivated as you write on through the middle of your novel and beyond.

Fiction Mission Statements

The idea of creating a mission statement for a novel or other fiction isn't original to me. I began thinking about it while reading Kristine Kathryn Rusch's book *Creating Your Author Brand*. Rusch shares her overall author mission statement: *All genres all the time.* It makes clear that she likes to write in multiple genres.

She also has one for each of her pen names. For Kristine Grayson, for example, the statement is *It's Not Easy To Have A Fairy Tale Ending.* In Rusch's words, that tells readers that "Grayson will always be goofy paranormal with a touch of romance, usually focusing on myths or fairy tales or both."

This book isn't about marketing. But putting together a mission statement can help you get in touch with what you love about your novel which can keep you writing on. It has been a huge help for me when I've had doubts.

My Mystery Mission

I shifted from supernatural thrillers to mysteries as my reading tastes shifted. But I chose the specific main character, genre, setting, and types of crimes for more specific reasons:

- I'm tired of mysteries, thrillers, and suspense novels that show women being tortured or victimized.

While I still read these types of books if the violence doesn't feel gratuitous, it isn't what I wanted to write. I personally feel the world is overloaded with stories in all forms that essentially warn women to fear strangers and new places and stay home and stay safe. Yet, the biggest danger in real life to women, statistically speaking, isn't the strangers outside their homes, it's the men closest to them in their lives.

That's why I chose to write about crimes committed by someone who knows the victim, and why my victims are more often male than female.

Also, the novels are told in first person, and the protagonist is a smart, determined, empathetic woman lawyer. The reader sees the story through her eyes as she tries to unravel the clues, not through the eyes of a victim being terrorized or a perpetrator committing the crime. That keeps the emphasis on solving the crime and seeking justice, not on the killer or the gory details of murder.

Readers have emailed me, and reviewers have pinpointed, how much they enjoy reading about a smart woman who solves crimes by using her wits, tapping into her connections, and listening to people. They also like a good murder mystery that's not gory or exploitative. When I hit a rough spot where I feel like my plot's not coming together, which happens at some point in the middle of each novel, I think about that and keep writing.

- I wanted to write about amazing and wonderful places in Chicago.

Whenever I travel and say I'm from Chicago, people mention the murder rate and wonder why I live here. While yes, my series is about solving murders, the novels highlight the very best parts of the city. Readers get to visit along with my characters great restaurants, outdoor artwork, a vibrant riverwalk, Lake Michigan, and all sorts of other fascinating and beautiful places.

- I believe most issues are complicated, and rarely is only one point of view completely right or wrong.

Showing many sides to issues and people matters to me. While in a murder mystery the villain generally is, well, a villain, I try to avoid black-and-white answers and characters who are all good or all bad. (A few slip in here and there, I admit.) The same goes for the issues that form the backdrop for the crimes.

The Charming Man, Book 2 in the Q.C. Davis mystery series, touches on immigration because a missing college girl may have let her student visa lapse, which makes her sister afraid to contact the police. That sets up a reason to come to my protagonist for help. The characters, however, rarely talk about immigration, as it only comes up if the plot requires it. All of them hold different views from one another, and none are presented as wonderful or terrible people simply based on what their views are on the subject.

I did something similar with certain religious issues in my Awakening supernatural thriller series which involves, in the first book, a supernatural pregnancy. In one of my favorite reviews, the reader said she liked the short scene where the main character considered an abortion, and loved that she couldn't tell what the author's views were on the issue.

While my main goal is to entertain, my hope is always that readers on any side of the issue will gain a little better understanding of a perspective unlike their own.

What's Your Mission?

For some writers, the idea of a mission statement or focusing on what your novel will do out in the world puts too much pressure on. If that's how you feel, you can set aside any idea about mission statements. You can return another time if you think it might be helpful, or skip it altogether.

But if you feel intrigued or neutral about the idea, give it a try. It can help you keep writing through challenging moments. And remember, you can always change it as your feel for your novel evolves.

Now let's talk about something that on the surface doesn't sound like a lot of fun, but can make your writing life so much more relaxed – creating a routine. And if you don't have a regular schedule, don't worry. It doesn't necessarily mean you need to write at the same time every day.

∽

Questions

- What do you love most about writing fiction?
- What matters most to you about writing a novel?
- Do you see themes that appear again and again in your fiction?
- Is there something specific you hope will come across to your readers through your novel?
- What makes you feel your novel matters in the world?

_____

_____

_____

_____

_____

_____

_____

_____

_____

14

WRITE MORE EASILY (ANY TIME) THROUGH ROUTINES

The common wisdom for writers is that you need to write every day and, ideally, at the same time every day. That works well for a lot of novelists, and I'll talk about it in this chapter. But if you can't do it, don't worry. It's not necessary.

The main reason so many writers and writing books pass on the write-every-day advice is that it is a good way to create a writing routine or habit. And it's our habits – what we do over and over – that get results, not what we do once in a while. As Napoleon Hill said, "...you are what your habits make you. And you can choose your habits." (From *Success Through A Positive Mental Attitude*, co-authored by W. Clement Stone.)

A habit goes a long way toward getting your brain accustomed to writing reliably whether you feel like it or not. With a habit, you don't need inspiration. The time comes and you write. You might not write as many words as you hoped, or you may feel what you write isn't particularly great, but you'll write something. And gradually those words will add up to a novel.

So let's talk about the different ways to form a habit. A set time is one way, and I'll talk about that first, but I'll get to others.

Telling Your Brain It's Time To Write

If your schedule is predictable and your physical and mental health allows, one of the easiest ways to create a routine that cues your brain that it's time to write is to follow that common wisdom. Pick a time each day when you can write. It could be a half hour or an hour before you go to work or before your kids gets up, your lunch hour if you get one, or a half hour before you leave your office when you shut your door and write.

If the same time each day isn't possible, try choosing the same time or times during the week. Figure out when it's most likely you'll be undisturbed. Maybe it's an hour or half hour every Sunday morning and Wednesday night. For a few years when I worked as a lawyer at a large and very busy firm, I was already getting up early and working late each day at law. The only time I was sure to have free on a regular basis was Friday nights because I could always get in early Saturday morning and work all day to finish whatever last-minute thing came up Friday afternoon. (Yes, this does say something about my social life.) I started small, with about forty-five minutes. Eventually I expanded to a few hours.

When the time you set aside rolls around, write during it even if you must write about how you don't have anything to write about. What you're doing is conditioning your brain that it's time to write. Just like you go to bed at a certain time or clock into work or wake your child for school at a particular time, now you'll write at a particular time. Eventually, whatever you start with, you'll find yourself writing about possible characters, story ideas, and scenes out of boredom if nothing else.

Once you have the habit, you can increase the amount of time you write, and the quality of what you write. Not only does that start conditioning your mind, it takes away all the decision-making. Rather than deciding if you'll write each day, you simply see what time it is and head for the keyboard or notebook.

If a routine time is impossible due to your schedule or health, though, you can set a routine through other signals to your brain.

Others Signals And Cues

Look for ways to create a routine that you'll always do along with your writing. Each time you sit down at the keyboard, for example, you might burn a specific scented candle. (I like chocolate-scented because it helps me relax. If it makes you go in search of a candy bar rather than write, you may want to try something else.)

Or make yourself a cup of a favorite flavor of tea or coffee and sip as you write. This has the added advantage of linking writing to something else you enjoy. Of course, whatever drink you choose, make sure it fits your time and diet. I started drinking entire pots of tea as I wrote and ended with acid reflux. Similarly, I generally avoid alcohol as part of a routine. It's too apt to make me lose focus, and I don't want an alcohol habit.

Clothing can also signal to your brain. Putting on your red socks or a super soft fleece can go with each writing session. Or, if it works for you, put on a suit or jeans and your favorite blazer. Whatever you want your writing uniform to be, it can tell your mind that it's time to write.

Playing certain music or nature sounds in the background can also be part of a routine if it doesn't distract you.

Even if you write at the same time every day or week, you may want to add one of the above into your routine to reinforce it. That can be especially useful if your writing time comes in the middle or at the end of a day filled with other projects. These signals can help you transition from one part of your day to the next.

How you routinely end your writing session also can make it easier to start next time.

Hook Yourself

When you near the finish of your writing time (or word count if you're writing until you hit that type of goal), make a point to set up your next writing session. Think of it as creating a hook for yourself.

Many novelists and creators of shows meant to be binge watched are great at doing this within their fiction. Most likely at some time in your life you've told yourself you'll only watch one episode of a show on a streaming service. Or that you'll read just one chapter of a novel before you go to sleep. But then the last chapter line or moment of the episode leaves a character hanging, introduces a new twist, or raises a question you must know the answer to. So you click Next Episode or turn the page.

The authors hooked you.

You can do the same thing to yourself. And the good news is you don't need to be nearly as dramatic (though it doesn't hurt). Simply use your last few minutes or fifty words to write a quick note on what you'll write in your next session. No need to labor over how you word your notes. You're the only one who will read them.

Here are some I've written:

- *Quille attends her first Seminar lecture, irritates the presenter by asking too many questions*
- *What's Oni's back story – why does she want to help Tara? What happened to her sister?*
- *Another body is found under the snow on the balcony. Or in the snow below the balcony? Hair sticks out like twigs*

It's a lot easier to write a note about what happens next, or a scene or character moment to explore, when you're already writing than it is to get started from a dead stop. So make life easier for future you by giving yourself a place to begin. It's like giving a car a push to get it started.

If you don't want to take time to make notes, you can also hook yourself by stopping in the middle of a scene. The next session you'll pick up exactly where you left off.

You can also do a little more mental preparation if you really want to speed ahead during your next writing session.

Write Like A Chef

Another way to ensure you write easily is to borrow from a chef's practice called *mise en place*. Think about any cooking show you've watched where the TV chef prepares a beautiful dish in ten minutes plus cooking time despite dozens of ingredients. Then you try it at home and it takes you at least forty-five minutes to be ready to pop the dish in the oven.

As you probably noticed, that's because before the cooking show started someone set out the pots, cooking utensils, and appliances, measured out the right amount of each ingredient, and chopped or diced whatever needed chopping and dicing.

That's *mise en place*, which literally translates to setting up, and it's another way to keep writing on.

Take a moment now to think about what you need to be ready to write the next scene in your novel.

- What characters will be in the scene?
- Does one of them still need a name?
- Is there a conflict between those characters? What is it?
- What happened in the most recent scene you wrote or outlined?
- Are there story questions your last few scenes left open?
- Where and when will the next scene take place?

_____

_____

_____

_____

_____

_____

_____

_____

_____

_____

_____

_____

_____

_____

—————————————————————
—————————————————————
—————————————————————
—————————————————————
—————————————————————
—————————————————————
—————————————————————
—————————————————————
—————————————————————
—————————————————————
—————————————————————
—————————————————————
—————————————————————
—————————————————————
—————————————————————
—————————————————————
—————————————————————
—————————————————————
—————————————————————
—————————————————————

You don't need to know the answers to all these questions. But knowing most of them will make it far easier and more fun to write when you get to your keyboard. You can ask these questions before you go to sleep at night, before you finish a writing session, while you're waiting to pick up your kids at school, or any other time when you can devote a little thought to your novel.

Then when the time you've set aside to write arrives, your fingers will likely fly across the keyboard.

Now that we've talked about forming a habit, let's discuss some day-to-day issues that can make it harder or easier to stick with it. Starting with your phone.

Questions

- Are there times you can set aside each week to write?
- What can you add to your routine as a signal to your brain to write?
- What are some hooks you imagine adding to the end of each writing session?

_____

_____

_____

_____

_____

_____

_____

_____

_____

_____

_____

_____

_____

15

YOUR PHONE AND YOUR WRITING

Your phone can help you focus on writing or it can distract you, as can other technology. The best way I've found to use my phone in a positive way to focus is to consciously choose these 3 things:

- Where the phone will live while I write
- Who can reach me while I write
- How long I will write in one stretch

Where To Put Your Phone

When you write, it's best to leave your phone in another room. Studies show that having a phone within reach, even if it's turned off, lowers our mental capacity for other things. Some part of our brain is always listening for the phone.

In fact, a study at the University of Texas at Austin found that people who put their phones in a separate room "significantly outperformed" study participants who kept their phones on their desks. They also slightly outperformed participants who put their phones out of sight in a bag or pocket.

I like to leave my phone on the bookcase in the hallway outside my home office. I feel more focused when I do that and often forget about time passing.

As a bonus, putting the phone far enough away that I must get out of my chair to reach it ensures that I'll move and stretch enough during my day.

Write Undisturbed

Most smartphones, in addition to a silent mode or button, have a setting called Do Not Disturb (or sometimes No Interruptions). This setting suppresses all alerts, including social media, and any notifications of texts, emails, and phone calls. When this setting is activated, your phone will not ring, make any other noise, or vibrate.

You can customize the setting to allow calls from certain numbers or repeat calls from the same number to come through. That way if, for instance, you're the person your aging grandmother depends on for a ride to the doctor or you need to answer a call from your child or anyone else, you won't miss the call. Or worry about missing important calls while you're writing.

Time To Focus

Now that you found a home for your phone and put it on Do Not Disturb or into silent mode, set its timer. (Or you can set any other type of timer that's handy.)

Choose a length of time to write that's short enough that you won't worry you're missing anything important by not taking calls or checking messages. But the block of time should be long enough that you can get something significant done on your current writing project.

For me, 30 minutes is ideal. After 30 minutes, I reset the timer for 3 to 5 minutes and stretch during that time. Doing so helps me alleviate aches and pains from sitting too long in one position. I also look at messages to be sure none requires an immediate response.

If I still have time in my day to write, I reset the timer for 30 minutes. You can repeat this process as many times as you want.

But even if you only write for one 15-30 minute block you will make progress.

Now let's talk about something trickier than phone and timers. People. Specifically, saying No to them. How to do it, when to do it, and why to do it, though not necessarily in that order.

Questions

- Do you know how to silence your phone or put it on Do Not Disturb?
- Where can put your phone so you can hear the timer or get to it in an emergency, but it's not in the room?
- What's the ideal amount of time to write undisturbed given your other responsibilities?

_____

_____

_____

_____

_____

_____

_____

_____

_____

_____

_____

16

YES TO WRITING AND NO TO...

It's much easier to put a phone on Silent than to say No to someone you care about who asks you to do something. But if you want to write novels, Saying No is key. Otherwise, you may never get beyond the first few chapters.

Do You Need To Say No More Often?

If you're often taking part in activities or doing favors "just this once" instead of writing, you may be having trouble saying No.

When I don't say No enough I start feeling not just stressed but angry. Angry at the demands on my time, angry at feeling out of control, angry at other people who keep asking me to do things.

And then I realize – it's up to me, not anyone else, to make the time I've chosen for writing my priority. Yes, there will be times it's not possible (more on that in Chapter 21), but it's still more my choice than anyone else's.

So how do you say No?

Getting Okay With No

In *Don't Sweat the Small Stuff and It's All Small Stuff: Simple Ways to Keep the Little Things from Taking Over Your Life*, author Richard Carlson says: "Just because someone throws you a ball doesn't mean you have to catch it."

This is important because most of us want to help other people. Helping is a huge part of how we survive as humans, and it has its own rewards. But if you tend to leap in, it's good to remind yourself that you don't always have to do so. Other people might be able to help just as much or more. In fact, who knows, you might be giving someone else an opportunity to shine if you back off.

Understand Your No

There are different reasons for wanting or needing to say No when asked to take on another task or project. Here are several:

1. It's something you really want to do but your schedule is overloaded already
2. Someone you care about asked, you want to help, but your schedule is already crowded
3. It's something you don't want to do regardless of your schedule but you feel you should do it
4. It's something you don't want to do for any reason

Which of the above is true affects whether you need to say No for all time, No with conditions, or Yes with conditions. Numbers 1-3 especially lend themselves to a qualified Yes, or a Yes If, rather than an out-and-out No.

Saying Yes If...

To decide if it makes sense to say a qualified Yes, ask yourself these questions:

- Is there a way to narrow or limit the task so that it fits your overall schedule and doesn't disrupt your writing time?
- Can you think of an alternate way to achieve the same goal that will take less time or effort?

For example, most semesters I teach legal writing to law students. They sometimes ask if I can help with advice on preparing for interviews or go over an article they've written. The demands of reviewing class work alone often make it hard to get my own writing and publishing done. But I want to help. It's the main reason I started teaching.

So often I answer with a condition: *Yes, I'd love to review your article if getting comments back to you in 3 weeks is soon enough.* Or: *Yes, I'm happy to give you advice if you can stay after class one evening (rather than needing me to meet at a separate time).*

If I can't make time to review an entire article, I might offer to do a narrower task such as meeting to discuss proposed topics or reviewing and marking a limited number of pages with suggested edits.

Other times I've offered an alternative, such as connecting the student with another lawyer who is more familiar with a particular area of law. (After I've checked to be sure that lawyer is willing to help.)

Think about something someone asked you to do recently where you wanted to take it on, but it would interfere with your writing. Can you propose an alternative?

Add some conditions?

Other times, though, you need or want to say No. Just No. Either because you don't see any way to fit in the new task in the near future without causing yourself a lot of pain or because it's something you truly have no desire or reason to do.

The key is to be clear.

Saying No Clearly

Saying No can be challenging. Especially if the person asking is someone you care about.

The key is to be clear so you don't get talked out of your No. Being clear means saying the word No without conditions. Or explanations. Why no conditions or explanations? As soon as you add either, you're inviting the person to come back with arguments about how you could get around those reasons and say Yes. Or with arguments about why your explanation isn't valid.

Here's how that usually goes:

You: Sorry, I can't come to dinner Sunday afternoon. That's my only time to write.

Family Member: That's okay – it'll only take a couple hours. You can write after. Or in the morning.

You: No, I can't. I've got budgets to prepare for work in the morning and plans in the evening.

Family Member: Can't you change your plans? And why are you working on the weekend anyway? You work too much.

You get the idea.

Instead, try saying: *No, it's not possible for me to be there Sunday. I hope to make it next time.*

When your family member (or whoever it is) pushes back and asks why or what you're doing, rather than get drawn in, simply rephrase your answer but say the same thing.

It's just not possible this weekend. I'm sorry to miss it and look forward to another time.

If the person keeps pressing, it's time to say that you need to go (hang up/leave/stop texting) but would love to talk again another time.

The Order Of No

The order in which you give your answer can help protect your relationship.

Notice above I suggested saying No (or it's not possible) first and then ending with a statement that lets the person know you care. That's because the word "but," even when it's implied as it is in the above examples, is very powerful. In fact, most of us only hear what comes after the "but."

Think about the classic "You're a great person, but..." No one thinks there's anything good coming after that. So, likewise, if you start with "I'd love to be there, but..." the listener will walk away thinking about the No.

If you flip the order, you're reassuring the person. Your words make it clearer that saying No is about your schedule, but you value and care about helping that person or being there.

We've talked about creating a writing routine and ways to make it more likely you'll devote time to your novel. But sometimes you've carved out the time and gotten in the habit of writing, but you're not making progress.

If that's happening, you may need to spend some time on discovery. Which is what the next chapter's about.

∾

Questions

- What's one thing you said Yes to that you later wished you hadn't?
- How will you handle a similar request in the future?
- Imagine yourself saying an unqualified No to someone who asks you for a favor. How will you phrase your No?
- How do you feel about that?

_____
_____
_____
_____
_____
_____
_____
_____
_____
_____
_____
_____
_____
_____
_____
_____
_____

17

MAKE TIME FOR DISCOVERY

We've all had it happen. You've chosen an idea for your novel and enjoyed writing those early chapters. Maybe you sped through them. But now you're at the end of a scene or chapter, or maybe in the middle of one, and you can't seem to go on.

You might stare at the screen for a while. Maybe walk away for five minutes, get a cup of coffee or tea, and come back. Or you take your dog for a walk.

Yet you still don't know what to write next. Or, worse, you think you do know but for whatever reason you're not sitting down to write it.

It may be that you need more time for discovery. It's very much like the process for generating novel ideas that I talked about in Part I. But now you know your big picture idea for your plot, or at least you've written a good chunk of your novel. This phase is to sort through the rest of your major plot turns and/or to fill in subplots, specific scenes, character arcs, theme. All the things that make a novel rich and powerful.

And all things that help you speed from one scene to the next to the next.

Outside Of Conscious Planning

As I've talked about, I lean toward the planner side when it comes to novel writing. Once I have my overall plot in mind, I first draft pretty quickly. But when I started shifting more and more of my work life to writing I discovered something surprising. Having three times the number of hours to devote to writing didn't mean I tripled the speed at which I finished a first draft.

That's because I hadn't realized that unconsciously, while working many hours at law, I also sorted out parts of my novel. It happened in odd moments, including the downtime I talked about in earlier chapters. At court while waiting for my case to be called or in line at a Corner Bakery, I mulled over parts of my plot or back story for my characters.

I thought of what I was doing as daydreaming. A way to entertain myself when I was bored and to feel I was making progress on my novel despite having little time to put words on the page.

What I didn't realize was it wasn't just an illusion to make myself feel better. I really was making progress on my novel, and that enabled me to jump right in when I did have time at the keyboard.

Here are some ways to do it on purpose.

Read More Non-Fiction

This reading is different from general reading to find ideas, yet it's not research on specific topics. It's more looking at big picture topics and themes that could fill in the blanks so you have more options for plot twists and character development.

For the second mystery in my Q.C. Davis series I read websites aimed at immigrants to the U.S. from various countries and paid attention to newspaper articles about immigration. Very little of that research made its way into the book. But it did inspire a suspect. He runs an immigration clinic in the apartment complex where my protagonist, many suspects, and the murderer are trapped during a blizzard.

I also read books about causes of death, as there are multiple murders in that novel. For the next mystery in the series, I read widely about charismatic, cult-like leaders and the self-improvement industry. I also listened to a podcast devoted to multi-level marketing (MLM) companies.

Images Of People And Places

As you did when generating ideas, you can page through magazines. But this time you're looking for photos of people who look like one of your characters or call to you for some other reason. You can also search for settings for the novel or things your characters might like or keep in their homes.

On the corkboard in my office, I still keep a photo of a magazine page that inspired the character of Erik Holmes, a wealthy CEO with an obsession about the end of the world and obscure religious cults in my Awakening series.

You can do the same thing but online through sites like Instagram and Pinterest. Pinterest has an added advantage of providing an online place to save and organize photos that relate to your books.

Documentaries

As with when you were looking for big picture ideas for your novel, watching documentaries is great for prompting ideas for scenes and helping fix plot holes.

Though I had no plan of including snake handling in my *Awakening* series, I happened to see a documentary on it. It solved an issue I had, which was how to put my protagonist in great danger without it being clear who was behind it. I chose a part of the country where snake handling was still practiced and plunged her into an underground cavern filled with rattlesnakes.

Music

Many writers create collections of songs or playlists that fit their stories or characters.

It doesn't mean that these songs would need to be played as a soundtrack if your book were a movie, though you can create a soundtrack if you like. But they are songs that suit a particular mood or character.

Choosing them helps me figure out how the characters feel and what's happening in their lives.

Free Writing/Talking

I like to scribble in a notebook or on scratch paper, or type quickly into a document, random thoughts about my story and characters. Often I never look at these notes again. The thoughts might or might not be directly related to the story. It's a way to hang out with my characters or explore how possible twists and turns might affect them. Sometimes rather than writing, I pace and talk.

Attending Events

As I talked about in Part 1, concerts, art exhibits, garden or city walks, sporting events, and just about anything you attend that stimulates your mind and helps you relax can also be part of the discovery process. All trigger emotions and set your mind free to wander.

It doesn't matter if you love the event of not. Some of my best ideas for characters and plot developments came to me while sitting through a concert that bored me nearly to tears. (No, I won't say what band was playing.)

Your Backburner

Another way to think about discovery is to imagine setting your novel, wherever you're at with it, into a pot of water on the back burner of the stove to let it simmer. The pot of water is your unconscious mind. As discussed in Part 1, it often sorts through things while you think about something else.

If you're a *Mad Men* fan, think about advertising star Don Draper telling his protegee Peggy Olsen how to come up with an idea for ad copy when she felt stuck. He said to think really hard about it, then forget it. That's why the two of them often went to movies when stuck.

You can make this part of your discovery process, too. Think hard about where you're at in your novel, then turn to one of the activities in this chapter or that we talked about in Part 1. While you're doing those things, your unconscious mind will make connections and come up with entirely new thoughts.

Ones you never would have imagined if you sat staring at the blank screen.

Why Do It

Embracing the discovery process can help ensure your words flow freely when you get to your keyboard. It can also prompt you to delve more deeply into your characters.

With my first mystery I had what I thought was a pretty solid first third of the book finished and a rough draft of the rest. To my surprise, when I sent it to my story editor her main response was that the mechanics of the plot seemed fine but, basically, who cares? She didn't understand why my protagonist did what she did or why it ought to matter to the reader.

Had I allowed myself more time for discovery, I likely would have developed more layered and engaging characters before plotting the book and writing the draft. But I didn't, so my rewriting process took three or four times as long as I'd expected.

Taking time to read and daydream and look at photos (or anything else from the above list) pushes me to really get to know my characters and consider different plot turns and twists I might have otherwise overlooked.

Though "push" is really the wrong word.

When I let myself spend time in discovery, I don't feel pushed at all. Instead, I feel relaxed and happy to be spending time with my characters in a place that isn't about hitting word counts. It reminds me of how I feel when I'm reading a novel I really love. It's as if I'm living in another world that's amazing, fascinating, and heart wrenching.

If that's the experience I want my readers to have, and it is, I need to be able to go there myself first. When I do, the words flow so much more easily, and I take so much joy in writing.

In the next chapter, I'll talk about some specific points you can think about as part of the discovery process. And the great thing is that you can start sorting through each in as little as 15 minutes.

Questions

- Do you know what your key characters look like?
- Where might you find photos of people to spark your imagination?
- What type of music might best suit your novel's storyline?
- Does your protagonist like that same type of music?
- What are some topics you could read about that might inspire plot twists?

_____

_____

_____

_____

_____

_____

_____

_____

_____

_____

_____

_____

_____

_____

_____

_____

_____

_____

_____

_____

_____

_____

_____

_____

_____

18

TWELVE THINGS IN FIFTEEN MINUTES

I love to write for long stretches of time. It gives me the chance to sink into my fictional world, which I enjoy. Doing that also helps me develop my characters in more depth and make connections between scenes and plot turns. But so can very short bursts of time that you use for discovery. That's because you can start sorting through a story element or question during that time. Then your unconscious mind will keep working on it as you go through the rest of your day or week. When you do sit down to write, your work will flow far more quickly and easily.

So here are 12 suggestions for what to sort through or start on in 15 minutes:

1. Scenes And Character Goals

Think about a scene you're struggling with. What does each character in the scene want? If the characters' goals don't conflict with one another, change one goal so it does and reimagine the scene. Try out any idea for the new goal, no matter how out there. It's only 15 minutes.

2. Sensing The Next Scene

Imagine the next scene you're planning to write or any scene

in your novel. You probably see it, right? Now engage all your senses.

What do you hear? What do you smell? If your character is eating, how does the food taste? What can your character(s) feel? Is the air warm, freezing, humid? Not all aspects of the sense will go into the scene when you write it. But this exercise allows you to hone in on the most vivid or the ones that most quickly draw your reader into the scene.

You might also learn something about your character as you delve into the sensory experience.

3. A New Perspective

Remember the last scene you wrote. Imagine that scene from a different character's point of view.

You may discover it works better. If it doesn't, or if your novel is told from only one character's point of view and you don't intend to change that, you'll still have gotten an important perspective on the scene. It will make your original viewpoint richer and may give you more plot and character ideas.

4. Protagonist Blocks

Brainstorm (or write down) three obstacles that block your protagonist from achieving her or his main goal in the novel. Consider ways your protagonist can get around each one. Also, ask yourself what your antagonist can do to make each obstacle more challenging for the protagonist.

5. Antagonist Blocks

Now brainstorm or write three obstacles in your antagonist's way. If your protagonist can be the driving force for them, all the better.

6. Date Your Protagonist

Imagine your protagonist on a 30-minute coffee date with someone she or he wants to make a good impression on. What are three things your protagonist would make a point to avoid saying about herself or himself? What three things would your protagonist be sure to mention?

7. An Antagonist Date

What might your antagonist say or not say on a date? As you did with your protagonist, imagine your antagonist on a get-to-know-you date with a stranger. Or, if you really want to have fun, imagine your protagonist and antagonist as strangers on a date with each other.

8. Side characters

Try the obstacles or coffee date with a key side character. You might want to explore more minor characters this way, too.

9. Think About Commitments And Reversals.

As we'll talk about more in the next chapter, the Midpoint of a novel challenges many writers. A Midpoint typically requires a major commitment or vow from the main character or a major reversal. The novel and movie *Gone With The Wind* raises many troubling issues, including as to how the Civil War and race relations are depicted. If you can read or watch the Midpoint of it, though, you'll see a scene where protagonist Scarlett O'Hara, near starvation, discovers no edible food in her neighbor's garden and vows as God as her witness to never be hungry again. It's a perfect example of a major commitment that drives the entire second half of the plot.

Brainstorm ways your character could make a true commitment or suffer a major reversal at the Midpoint of your novel.

10. Beginning Lines

Brainstorm first lines for your novel. If you're having trouble, check out first lines of novels you've loved, search for classic first lines on your phone or laptop for inspiration, or look at books on your shelves if you have access to them right now. Do any of them give you ideas for your first line?

11. First Scenes

Think about the first scene of your novel (whether you've written it yet or not) that features your protagonist. What does the protagonist want in that scene and what is blocking getting it? If you're not sure, experiment with different options. If you know, come up with three ways to make the character's goal more significant or life-changing.

12. Chapter Endings

Brainstorm strong chapter endings. A good chapter ending urges the reader on to the next chapter. This can be a hint of things to come, an open question (why is the police detective calling the protagonist?), or a genuine cliffhanger.

Using These Suggestions

You can think or write about most of the above suggestions wherever you are – standing in line, riding a bus, waiting to pick up your child from school, walking to or from the store (though be careful not to bump into anyone).

Even if all you do is think about one of these for 15 minutes, you'll have made progress on your novel. Also, when you do get to your keyboard, whether it's for 15 minutes or a longer time, you'll be ready to jump in and write the next scene.

I've been talking generally about keeping the ball rolling during the middle section of your novel. But there are some specific concerns about the halfway mark of a novel that cause many writers to falter. And that's what the next chapter covers.

Questions

- Which of these 12 suggestions have you tried?
- When are you most likely to have 15 minutes free?
- Are there other questions or issues that you could start sorting out in 15 minutes?

_____

_____

_____

_____

_____

_____

_____

_____

_____

_____

_____

_____

_____

_____

_____

_____

_____

_____

_____

_____

_____

_____

_____

_____

_____

_____

_____

_____

_____

_____

_____

_____

_____

_____

_____

19

STILL STUCK IN THE MIDDLE?

Whether you plot in detail, create a loose structure, or wing your zero draft, as you near the halfway point you may start feeling stuck. That's because many of us start a novel with a pretty clear idea of who our main characters are, where they're at in the beginning, and where we want them to end. We might also know some key developments. But as we go on, the plot starts to feel like nothing more than "and then this happens, and then this happens, and then this happens...."

Not only do you fear your reader will get bored, you may feel bored yourself. Which can lead to feeling blocked.

While this book isn't primarily about plotting, slumping or stalling in the middle often is about some part of your plot that's not quite strong enough to keep the momentum going. So let's talk about how to pinpoint the issue and address it.

Getting Rolling Again

The first step is to recognize why you've stalled. If you just don't feel like writing, but you know where you're going with the story and why, you may need to do more to create and maintain your writing habit. You also might be able to write through the slump by powering through the next scene and the next, setting aside your concerns about it. Reread the zero draft chapter if you need a push.

But if you're slowing or stopping because you're not sure what happens next in your novel, or you seriously doubt your planned plot turns will keep readers engaged, the issue isn't that something's blocking you from writing. It's not knowing what to write next. In that case, rather than force yourself to write a scene, any scene, switch gears to focus on your story.

The best way to do that varies from writer to writer and may differ from one novel to another, but below are some methods you can try. I've used most of these, and some you'll remember from earlier in this book:

- Reread your last scene and, rather than try to write the next one, write or type the words *What if*. Write about an option, any option, as if you're simply writing a note to yourself. Write 10 or 20 *What ifs*. When one rings true to you, write that scene even if it's not what you originally planned. Repeat with the next scene if you need to.
- Consider your protagonist's goal for the novel. Is it a strong goal? How hard is it to reach? What obstacles must the protagonist overcome to reach it? Now make each obstacle more challenging. Or make the goal larger. Or both.
- Do the same with your antagonist's goal. Keep in mind the antagonist's goal should directly contradict the protagonist's – if one wins, the other loses. If that's not the case, can you make it so? How might that play out?
- Free write, or talk out loud to yourself, about what you think your main character, antagonist, or any key character might do throughout the novel that will create more conflict and tension.
- Ask yourself, out loud or in writing, what the next worst thing is that could happen to your protagonist. And then the next worst thing after that and then the next. Ask the

same question for other characters, including the antagonist.

- Interview in your mind (or on paper or out loud) key characters about who they are, what they want, and why. Push them to give you real answers, including ones they may try to hide from themselves.
- Spend the next several writing sessions writing out your major plot turns or, if you've already done that, creating a detailed outline or revising it if you already created one. Start from wherever you are in the novel right now.
- If you're truly unsure about how to plot the rest of your novel, use some of your writing time to read books on plotting and try one of the methods in those books.

I suggest you at least sketch out some key plot points, because whether you like outlines or not most writers need some sense of where they're going to keep writing through the middle of the novel. Because that's where so many writers struggle, if you outline nothing else, it's worth spending time on what happens at the halfway mark, or Midpoint, of your novel.

_____

_____

_____

_____

_____

_____

_____

_____

Below is how I approach it. This way of looking at the Midpoint adapts to any genre, including literary novels. You may find it doesn't work for you while another plotting approach does. But if you read it, at the very least it should give you ideas on what else you might do with your story.

And once you understand it, you'll likely be able to see it in almost any movie, television episode, or novel you've loved.

The Middle Matters Most

I learned this structure from a screenwriting friend, and I alluded to it in the last chapter when I mentioned the halfway mark in _Gone With The Wind_.

At the Midpoint of your novel, your protagonist should make a major commitment, suffer a major reversal, or both. This changes the entire course of the story because in the first half of a novel the protagonist mainly responds to two major plot points. The Inciting Incident – the event that sets your main plot in motion – and the first major plot turn, which typically comes from outside the protagonist, raises the stakes, and spins the story in a new direction.

At the Midpoint, though, the protagonist stops getting spun and takes charge, throwing caution to the wind and committing in full to the quest. Or the protagonist suffers a major reversal that essentially requires doing the same thing.

As an example, in my favorite movie of all time, _The Terminator_ – spoiler warning if you've never seen it – protagonist Sarah Connor has been on the run from someone she believes is a human being intent on killing everyone named Sarah Connor. She takes shelter in a police station, believing the detective who questions her that the man's seemingly superhuman strength is a result of drug use and that the police can protect her. Sarah rejects what her ally, a man named Reese, told her, which is that a cyborg from the future is after her because she'll become the mother of a future key resistance fighter.

But she suffers a major reversal when the cyborg invades the police station killing nearly everyone in his hunt for Sarah. And she commits fully to the quest when she joins in with Reese, completely buying into his story about the future.

As another example of a reversal, in the movie *Toy Story* – more spoilers coming! – two toys, Sheriff Woody and Buzz Lightyear, are at odds for the first half of the film. In fact, Woody's jealousy of Buzz Lightyear leads to both of them getting lost far from home. At the Midpoint, though, everything gets a hundred times worse.

Both Buzz and Woody get stuck in an arcade game where the gamer can grab toys out of a bin with a metal claw. The dreaded Sid, a boy who tortures and dismembers toys, grabs Buzz. Woody tries to save Buzz, but instead gets carried out along with him into Sid's clutches.

Now not only are both toys far from home, the evil toy torturer has captured them. To make things worse, Sid's other toys surround and scare Woody and Buzz, and both lose faith in their ability to get away.

This Midpoint capture is a major reversal for Woody. He also made a commitment by trying to help Buzz despite all his jealousy.

In both examples, as well as in *Gone With The Wind*, the protagonists shift gears entirely, become more active, and drive the story forward for the second half.

For more examples of Midpoints, check your favorite books or movies. See what happens halfway through. You'll almost always see the protagonist make a major commitment or suffer a major reversal from which the protagonist now struggles to recover.

Finding Your Midpoint

You can free write or talk through options about your Midpoint.

It's also a great time to do the What If exercise. Play out the different ideas in your mind to see which one creates a reversal, leads to the main character making a vow and committing to the quest, or both. Whatever method you use, once you know your Midpoint you'll find it much easier to write on from there.

You may find that you need to adjust what you've written so far to set the stage for a strong Midpoint. My advice, is to make a note of that but keep writing from your Midpoint forward as if you already made the change. That way you can see how well it works and won't get mired in rewriting the first half of the book before you finish.

Now that we've talked about your protagonist committing, let's talk about you. Because strengthening your commitment can make it much more likely you'll get through the middle and finish your novel.

~

Questions

- How can your protagonist commit to the quest or goal?
- Once your protagonist commits, how will that change her/his/its choices and actions from then on?
- What does your protagonist want most as you near the middle of the novel?
- What could your antagonist do to block the protagonist and cause a major reversal?
- Write 10 or 12 What Ifs. Which one excites you the most?
- Which one suits your story?

_____
_____
_____

_____

_____

_____

_____

_____

_____

_____

_____

_____

_____

_____

_____

_____

_____

_____

_____

20

ARE YOU COMMITTED OR JUST INTERESTED?

Quite often when I tell a new acquaintance I'm a writer, the person responds by telling me that's fantastic because they have a terrific idea for a novel. They can tell me about it, and I can write it. Usually people are puzzled when I don't jump at the chance. But while coming up with an idea can be a challenge at first, that phase of writing typically takes the least amount of time.

What takes more effort and determination is skipping whatever it is you've decided to skip, rearranging your life, and investing a lot of time writing a novel that might or might not ever matter to anyone but you.

Which means that no matter how much you love to write, and I do, there'll be moments you'll long to drop onto your couch instead. Or when you'll be pulled in all directions and feel guilty if you write instead of going to that family dinner, or cooking that family dinner, or sewing a costume rather than buying one for your child's first Halloween.

The reality is that a lot of people have great ideas for novels. And a lot of people take writing classes or workshops, start novels, or write a few scenes here and there. But very few start a novel, and fewer finish it.

Why? Because while many people are interested in writing a novel, few commit to it.

Commitment v. Interest

I'm a huge Tony Robbins fan. (Based on his books, not his conferences, which are a bit too pricey for me.) One distinction Robbins makes that's key to writing is commitment versus interest.

If you're interested in doing something, you probably admire or envy other people who've achieved that goal or engaged in that activity. You believe you'd enjoy it, maybe you find it fun or fulfilling when you do it, and you feel it's something you'd be proud of.

But if you don't do it, other than feeling a little regret it won't seriously upset you.

For example, let's say you took piano lessons as a kid. As an adult, you might wish you had kept practicing and you might include "play piano more often" as one of your New Year's resolutions or goals.

But if, despite that resolution, during the next twelve months your piano is mostly used to display family photos (or photos plus a favorite china tea set and some bottles of wine, not that that's what I use mine for), you're interested in playing piano, but you're not committed to it.

On the other hand, if you're committed, playing piano and playing it well matters to you more than almost anything else. If life gets busy, you'll push aside another task to make time to play. If you feel sick, but not truly awful, you'll sit at the keyboard even if it's for five minutes. Or, if that's too hard, you'll lie on your couch and practice your fingering in your mind or listen to music you can learn from.

As it is with piano playing, so it is with writing a novel.

Committing To Writing A Novel

If, despite your best laid plans (and absent serious illness or other life circumstances that prevent you from all types of work), you never get more than a few scenes or chapters written, you may need to shift from interest to commitment.

Here are some ways to do that:

1. Set a deadline

Without a deadline, it's easy to imagine you'll write next week or next month. Then you turn around a year later and you've still not finished your novel.

So choose a date by which you'll finish a solid first draft of your book, a draft you can show to someone you trust to give you useful feedback. Pick a date that's reasonable but a little ambitious so you'll need to make an effort to find the time. It could be six months, a year, or two years down the road.

2. Write down all the reasons you want to finish a novel

Here you can think back to your mission statement or simply write all the other reasons that come to mind.

Maybe you've had an idea for a novel forever that you believe is perfect, and you so want to see how it plays out. Or you love immersing yourself in a fictional world, and you want that feeling more often. Perhaps you imagine being interviewed on a podcast or television show, speaking at a conference, or reading from your novel at a launch party.

_____

_____

_____

_____

_____

_____

_____

_____

_____

_____

_____

_____

_____

_____

_____

_____

_____

_____

_____

_____

_____

_____

Once you've written your reasons, spend a few minutes on each one imagining how you'll feel if all of that comes true. You can do this before you fall asleep at night if you're pressed for time. Makes you feel pretty great, right?

3. Imagine yourself a year down the road and you haven't written a word

Now imagine instead that it's a year later and you've made no progress on your novel. How does that feel?

Compare it to the feelings you had when you imagined reaching your goals. Write that down. Add the other downsides of not finishing your novel. Will you be embarrassed to tell other people you never finished (or never started)? Feel envious every time you pass a bookstore or get a notice of a new release from a favorite author?

_____

_____

_____

_____

_____

_____

_____

_____

_____

_____

_____

_____

_____

_____

_____

_____

4. Tell other people about your goal

Tell three people that you will finish a novel within six months, a year, two years, or whatever your timeline is. Just saying it aloud to witnesses strengthens your commitment. Even if you never speak of it again and all three people forget about it, you'll know that if they do happen to ask and you haven't written a word you'll have to admit that. (Or lie, but you wouldn't do that, right? And, anyway, you'll know the truth no matter what you say.)

If you tend toward being an Obligor, as we talked about in Chapter 12, this strategy can be especially useful. But it strengthens commitment for most other writers, too.

5. Ask for help.

This step goes one beyond telling people to enlisting others in your goal.

Ask a friend or family member to check in with you once a month and ask how the novel is going. You don't need to give detailed answers. But knowing you'll be reporting what you did or didn't do will add to your commitment to have something positive to say, even if it's only "wrote a hundred words" or "figured out who my antagonist is."

All these strategies can help you commit. And in Part 3, Crossing the Finish Line, we'll talk about more day-to-day ways to ensure that you write. Before we get there, though, let's take a moment to talk about coping with life events that take you away from writing for a while.

Questions

- Do you feel you're committed to writing a novel rather than merely interested?
- If not, which of the above strategies sounds most like it will help you commit?
- Who might you enlist to aid you in reaching your goal?
- How will you feel when you finish your novel?

_____

_____

_____

_____

_____

_____

_____

_____

_____

_____

_____

_____

_____

_____

_____

_____

_____

_____

_____

_____

_____

_____

_____

_____

_____

21

CURVE BALLS, OFF RAMPS, AND WHEN TO BE FLEXIBLE

Maybe you started your novel, outlined it, or wrote some scenes or character sketches. You're all set to first draft, or you finished the first half, and the unexpected happens.

A flood damages your home, you need to care for an ill friend or family member, you become injured yourself. In addition to your grief and learning to cope with the change in your life, you may feel more frustrated, depressed, or anxious because you can't write or aren't progressing the way you feel you "should."

It's tempting to say just write anyway. After all, you're committed, right?

But there may well be times in life when writing anyway, or writing as much as you normally do, just isn't possible for various reasons. Many writers are fortunate enough to be generally well much of their lives but nonetheless go through periods where their mental, physical, and emotional health limits whether and how much they can write. Others live with chronic conditions that make any type of work or pursuit, including writing, far more difficult if not seemingly impossible.

I've dealt with these types of challenges, and this chapter includes my suggestions for getting through without getting stuck.

As with all the advice here, though, keep in mind that what was most useful for me might not be the best approach for you. Also, I'm not a doctor or health professional, and this is not medical, psychological, or psychiatric advice. If you need assistance with your well-being, I hope you'll reach out to the appropriate professional.

You Don't Write With Your Toes, But...

A few years ago in late April, I broke two bones in my foot. One was a major bone, so instead of a walking boot for a short time (as one of my friends had for a stress fracture), I had to stay off my foot entirely for over 10 weeks and wore a series of different casts that reached to my knee. After that I wore a walking brace and was still rehabbing nearly a year later.

When the doctor first told me the treatment plan, I figured it wouldn't interfere with my writing. After all, I don't write with my toes.

But it turned out wearing a cast made it hard to find a comfortable way to sleep, sit at a desk, or get around inside or outside. Things like brushing my teeth and making the bed took twice if not three times as long as usual on crutches. And I was exhausted. Not only from lack of sleep but because it takes a lot of energy for your body to heal.

Though my fingers could still type, I didn't write all that much for the first 6-8 weeks. But I learned a lot about dealing with curve balls that affect your writing.

An Off Ramp Is Not Forever

It can help to think of these types of one-time events as an off-ramp from the expressway (or a freeway or highway, depending on where you live). You're taking a temporary detour, but you'll get back on eventually. And sure, maybe it'll take a little longer to get where you meant to go. But you may very well have some experiences that will make your novel richer for it.

If you can keep your writing schedule and it helps you feel better to do it, then go ahead. If not, though, remind yourself that it's okay to do less. As Anthony Robbins says in *Awaken The Giant*

Within, most people overestimate what they can do in one year and vastly under estimate what they can do in ten. Finishing a novel is a long game, and while over time there'll likely be more than one off-ramp, you can still get to your destination.

Do Something Different

Often you can still move forward with your writing if you shift to a different phase or take an alternate approach.

During the first few weeks of my recovery, I found it hard to summon the energy to write or read much. But I did two things that ultimately helped me feel better and sparked new ideas.

Each time I iced my foot I watched a segment of the Lizzie Bennet Diaries, a modern-day take on my favorite book of all time, *Pride and Prejudice*, told as a video blog. In doing so, I engaged with a new (to me) form of storytelling and delighted in a different spin on a story I loved.

Once I was doing better, I used *Pride and Prejudice* as an example for plot points when I recorded an updated audiobook edition of my book *The One-Year Novelist: A Week-By-Week Guide To Finishing Your Novel In One Year*. And while revisiting the story I loved told in a new way didn't change my next novel, it did influence a later mystery I wrote where the protagonist learns about the murder victim partly through her YouTube videos.

Focus On Parts Of Your Novel

I also engaged in a lot of the types of thought experiments and imaginings discussed in Chapter 17 about Discovery.

If something happens that keeps you from writing or finishing your novel right now, you may be able to write pieces that build toward that novel all the same. You can write about a character, a scene, or a potential plot turn. If writing's too hard, try doing something else to help create or plan your story, such as imagining a scene or interviewing a character in your mind.

It's easy to think about what you're not doing. But rather than thinking about the hours you don't spend writing in a day or week, give yourself credit for the fifteen minutes you do.

All of this background work may enable you to speed ahead

faster when you can write again. And it almost certainly will make your writing richer and more layered.

But what about more serious issues? Ones that won't be resolved in a matter of weeks or months?

Writing When Not Well

My first experience with a chronic condition started in my twenties. I developed tendinitis in my hands, wrists, and arms. At the time (in the early 1990s), there wasn't a lot of awareness of carpal tunnel syndrome, tendinitis, or other RSIs (repetitive stress injuries) from keyboarding. My fingers went numb during the night, my hands and wrists tingled, and pain shot up my arms from my hands. Yet a lot of people implied or outright said that it was all in my head or due to stress. The suggestion that I could somehow fix myself simply by relaxing only made me feel worse.

The doctor I saw through the company's workers compensation policy told me to keep working unless or until there was nerve damage. Then I could have surgery, which was the only real treatment option at the time.

That struck me as a phenomenally bad idea.

I quit my office job and moved home to my parents' house in the hope that a few months of not working would help my hands heal. Instead, I plunged into depression and anxiety.

Not Working, Not Writing, Not Functioning

For the first four or five weeks home, I found it hard to get out of bed. Once I did, I lay on the couch and watched television until the late afternoon.

I struggled to figure out some other type of job I could do to support myself again. All my work experience, though, had to do with typing and computers. And writing, and playing guitar, the other creative pursuit I loved, hurt my hands.

I felt worthless.

The main things that I thought of as being who I was — a musician, writer, and a hard worker — had all been taken from me. And I didn't know how to get them back. (All of this also coincided with a break up with my boyfriend of six years, so I'd also lost my primary relationship.)

In one way, whether I could write fiction or not "should" have been the least of my worries. I hadn't made any money writing by then, so it wouldn't help me back to living on my own and supporting myself.

Yet after my fear that I'd never be able to move out of my parents' house again was my fear that I wouldn't be able to write. Without writing, I wasn't sure who I was or how much I'd get out of life.

More To Life Than Writing

If I could go back, I'd tell myself that to love writing and to write can be a wonderful thing, but sometimes other things need to take priority. Things like physical, emotional, and mental health. I felt I had to figure out all at once (a) all my health issues, (b) a new occupation, and (c) how I'd ever write again without severe pain. And I felt like a failure because I couldn't.

Now I'd tell myself that before I could write I needed to be sure I kept breathing and stayed alive. If I was able to write and it helped me do that, great. If writing made me feel worse, though, then it was okay, and quite possibly necessary, to mentally set it aside for a while and focus on whatever would help me keep functioning.

No Overnight Fixes

While I rarely feel the sort of depression and anxiety I experienced during the year and a half I moved back in with my parents, I've had a few rough times. It's like a broken bone that hasn't quite mended. Stepping a certain way or falling sometimes breaks it again.

And though my fingers rarely grow numb, if I'm at the keyboard too long my hands still get sore despite the many accommodations I've made over the years.

The hardest part of all of it was that I kept wanting to wake up one day and have my old life back. I only started to feel better emotionally and mentally when I realized that wasn't happening. That the only place I could start from was where I was.

Accommodations And Work-Arounds

In the long run, my need to find a new type of work prompted me to retrain to become a paralegal, and that led to becoming a lawyer. As a result, a decade later, I was far better off financially and professionally than I had been when I developed the tendinitis. And, as I talked about earlier in this book, much of the experience fed into my novels and made my writing more layered in the long run.

For the physical aspect of writing, and generally to deal with my on-going hand, wrist, and arm pain, I made dozens if not hundreds of small changes. For example, I use an ergonomic keyboard and separate monitor I plug into my laptop and an adjustable desk, take breaks every 30 minutes to stretch, and dictate first drafts rather than type them.

When my RSI bothered me the most, I wrote in very short bursts. I also engaged in the discovery activities I talked about above rather than writing.

Some of these strategies came in handy later when physically I could write longer but I had far less free time.

Flexible Writing Goals

Whether you're dealing with a temporary off ramp or a long-term challenge, it also can help to break your novel writing into smaller goals. And, sometimes, to let go of goals altogether if you need more flexibility.

During the worst of my depression, for example, I didn't set writing goals. If it made me feel better to write, then I wrote. Otherwise, I didn't. When my depression became more manageable and my tendinitis was slightly better, so that I could work at a job though still in a lot of pain, I started writing in a journal. Later, when I did start another novel I didn't worry about when I would be done. I just aimed to finish at some point. That was unusual for me, because I love lists and plans.

In the darkest times, though, lists and plans made me feel worse. They emphasized what I felt I "should" be doing and couldn't. They can be useful tools, but they're not the right ones for every circumstance.

If you're struggling with physical or mental health issues, flexibility is key. If you can still write and it helps you, great. If you need to set aside your novel to address your health issues, or you feel better when you do, that's okay too. You can try some of those discovery tasks or just return to your novel another time.

I hope this chapter and some of my experiences give you ideas or inspiration if you're struggling with injuries or health issues.

Now let's talk about finishing your novel.

Questions

- **What are some off-ramps you've experienced?**
- **How might you adjust your writing routine if you experienced an unexpected life event?**
- **Have you broken your goal of writing a novel down into smaller parts?**

_____
_____
_____
_____
_____
_____
_____
_____
_____
_____
_____
_____
_____

PART III

CROSSING THE FINISH LINE

22

STAYING THE COURSE

1. *You must write.*
2. *You must finish what you write.*

- Robert Heinlein's first two rules of writing

So far, we've talked about what I think of as stumbling blocks on the writing path that are pretty easy to identify, such as not knowing what to write next or needing to create a writing routine or habit. We've also covered more complicated challenges like dealing with injuries or illness. Hopefully you've found some of the exercises useful and explored getting more leverage on yourself.

But what if you've read to this point in the book, you're generally well, you chose an idea, found your writing space and time, and still you're staring at a blank page? Or maybe you've gotten your novel underway but often find yourself going back to rewrite the same scenes or chapters or rework your plot, barely moving forward for months or years. Or perhaps you're not rewriting, but jumping from project to project without ever finishing.

Most likely some fears and quite possibly some hopes are

undermining your momentum, making it harder to finish your novel.

That's what this section of the book is about. If you're someone who speeds to the end once it's in sight, you may feel this last part doesn't apply to you. You might find it helpful all the same, though. Some of the issues I talk about, including hopes and fear about writing, can also come into play earlier in the writing process, as can the suggestions for dealing with them.

If you are struggling, this chapter and the following ones should help you get to the finish line.

But, first, let's talk about why finishing matters, even if you've started to feel this particular novel isn't working and are tempted to try something else instead.

The Rewards Of Writing "The End"

I never met science fiction writer Robert Heinlein, but his rules about writing and finishing, quoted above, are among the first I ever heard about writing. While no rules apply to everyone all the time, finishing your novel is key to two things. The first is obvious. If you want to sell your novel to a publisher or directly to readers, you need to finish it. But second and less obvious is that whether or not you ever sell this particular novel, you'll learn hundreds if not thousands of times more by finishing it than if you stop.

For one thing, you'll learn how to finish a novel. And you'll learn much more about the pieces of a novel and how they form into a whole that engages a reader.

Also, you might very well discover that your draft is far better than you expected, or at least that you have much more to work with than your feelings at the moment indicate. But you'll never know unless you finish it.

The Last Leg

Almost every writer feels frustrated or despondent somewhere in the second half of a novel. Perhaps you wrote just beyond the middle and felt good about it, or you finished three-quarters of your zero draft, but now you're feeling doubt. You question your entire idea or wonder if anyone will care about your protagonist. Maybe you're unsure you started in the right place.

But those feelings rarely relate to how well the novel works or doesn't. You've simply spent enough hours that you're weary, much like a marathon runner might feel just past the midpoint of the race.

In fact, trying to evaluate the plot, the theme, the protagonist's growth, or almost any aspect of a novel as a whole can't truly be done unless it's, well, whole. Let's say it turns out your original idea wasn't large enough to sustain a novel. Maybe your protagonist needed a more challenging goal to make it work. Or the antagonist needs better motivation to throw more genuine obstacles at protagonist.

Those issue can all be improved when revising. Nearly all novelists revise their zero drafts more than once, sometimes extensively. So it's highly unlikely your idea (or your protagonist or theme or plot) will never work. And seeing what doesn't and fixing it not only improves your current novel, it will help you write a stronger zero draft of your next one.

Most of what's covered in Parts 1 and 2 can also help you in the last phase of your novel. If that's not enough to keep you going, though, some of your feelings and thoughts about yourself and your writing might be getting in the way.

So let's talk about those.

～

Questions

- **Do you have concerns about what might not be working in your novel so far?**
- **What are they?**
- **Which exercises and approaches from Parts 1 and 2 helped you the most?**
- **Do any of them apply now?**

- How do you feel about the idea of finishing your novel?

_____
_____
_____
_____
_____
_____
_____
_____
_____
_____
_____
_____
_____
_____
_____
_____
_____
_____
_____
_____
_____
_____
_____
_____
_____
_____
_____
_____
_____
_____

_____

_____

_____

_____

_____

_____

_____

_____

_____

_____

23

HOPES AND FEARS

If you've addressed the issues covered earlier in this book but still can't cross the finish line, or you often switch gears midstream to shift to a different project, fear may be getting in your way. Specifically, fear of success and of failure. Ironically, both can cause you to feel apprehensive about finishing your novel.

It's not always obvious what's going on, though, as these fears can take different forms.

Heads You Fail, Tails You Succeed

If you often ask yourself questions like the ones below, fearing you'll fail at writing may be getting in your way:

1. What if I spend a ton of time writing and I never finish?
2. Or I finish a novel and find out I'm no good at writing?
3. What if no one buys what I write?
4. Or I get bad reviews?

Success also can raise anxiety. Which seems strange, especially in a world that constantly tells us to set goals. Most of us are practically programmed to strive for success or admire people who achieve it. That can make it harder to spot those concerns. Rarely will your mind whisper, "Uh-oh, you might succeed at this!" But success has consequences, which can be positive or negative, including:

1. More people notice you
2. Your life changes
3. Success isn't all that you hoped it would be

Whether or not you think fear is an issue for you, I encourage you to read on. You might find fears you weren't consciously aware of. And even for the most confident person, fear sometimes works its way in. It can particularly affect writing because that's something that means so much to most novelists.

Below are some of the forms these fears – and sometimes your hopes – can take that may undermine your drive to finish your novel. If you identify with some or all of them, don't worry. I'll talk in the next chapter about how to address these concerns and write on.

Dashed Dreams

All your life, or at least since you decided to write fiction, you may have dreamed of seeing your book in your local bookstore or being interviewed by your favorite television personality about your novel. Or maybe you imagined book signings as a way to motivate yourself. Sometimes, though, these hopes backfire. Because as long as you don't finish a novel, you don't need to find out whether your hopes can be realized. You don't need to risk rejection or disappointment.

In short, you're free to keep daydreaming about what could happen someday without risking your dreams being dashed right now.

That's particularly scary if writing is big part of your identity.

Loss Of Identity

If you're like me, a large part of who you are (or who you feel you are) relates to being a writer. This identity can pose challenges because it's likely tied up with so much more than whether or what you write. It brings in your view, and society's view, of what a "writer" is. For many of us, this includes factors that rest mainly on other people, such as gaining a wide readership, earning money at writing, and critical response to our work.

As with the loss of a dream, if you finish a novel or several novels and don't achieve whatever you associate with being a novelist or writer, you may feel less entitled to claim your identity. In contrast, if you keep rewriting the first half of a novel or keep shifting projects, you can feel like you're shoring up your chances. After all, you're making sure you work is excellent or perfect before you put it out in the world.

Ironically, that can make it easier to keep feeling like a writer. Everyone knows writers have blocks from time to time, right? That's why it's called writer's block. You might even feel like more of a writer because clearly it's so important that you're willing to keep laboring over this one novel year after year.

Low Return On Investment

The questions at the beginning of this chapter highlight that writing a novel requires time and effort. It often requires investing money as well. You've probably taken classes or workshops, or at least bought books, to help learn your craft. You might attend writing conferences. If you didn't already have one, you probably bought some type of computer.

You could put your time, effort, and money toward some other pursuit. Rather than novel writing, you might meet new people, spend more times with loved ones, take a side job (with a better guarantee of income than writing), develop another career, or simply relax more. In the business world, this is what's known as an opportunity cost – losing one opportunity because you choose to devote time to another. Basically, you can't do everything, so when you choose writing you're choosing not to do something else.

This particular concern is a great example of how fears both of failing and succeeding come into play. You can fear both that you'll fail to ever finish a novel or that if you succeed at writing it the rewards won't be great enough to justify the time and money invested.

The End Of The World

Another consequence of finishing a novel is that it's finished. There's an obvious statement, right?

What I mean is that once you call your novel done, you're not living in that fictional world anymore. The characters you spent so much time with won't be your everyday companions. Sure, if you write a series, you may revisit them, but never in exactly the same way. The twists and turns they faced in this novel won't matter or take up your mind. Which leaves an empty place in your life.

The more novels you write, the less you'll feel that way at the end. But it is a real loss. Especially if the next step is sending those characters out into the world, perhaps to be judged and found wanting.

Being Judged

Finishing your novel and putting your work out into the world means people will read it and judge it. During the zero draft, you shut off the critical part of your brain. But once you finish that draft and start editing, you'll tap into it so you can improve your writing. Unfortunately, that same part of your brain also often offers unhelpful comments that reinforce your fears. Spotting a clunky dialogue line – something you can fix – is helpful. That voice telling you you're simply no good at this novel writing thing is not.

From there, it's easy to imagine that if you share your novel with the world all sorts of people will echo that voice. They'll comment on and critique your work. And those people include critics, reviewers, and possibly Internet trolls.

Most likely, they'll spot any errors you made. A typo, a research mistake, or a word usage that strikes them as incorrect. (And there will be at least one or two because you're human, and so are editors.) No one likes making mistakes. And it feels much worse for people to point them out in public. But if you send your novel out into the world, that's what you're signing up for.

You're also signing up for reviews. The more readers you gain, the more reviews you'll get. And because no book gets 100% fantastic reviews, the more readers you gain – the more success you have – the more negative feedback you'll get. That's another consequence of success that also correlates with fears of failure, if you view failure as anyone disliking or criticizing your work.

Being Seen

In addition to critiques of your work, if a lot of people read your novel you personally may become more visible to the world. That, too, can spark some anxiety.

Some writers fear being stalked in person or trolled on the Internet. Because the fear of strangers runs deep in many cultures, that type of anxiety about stalking can loom large despite that most published writers struggle not with being noticed but with getting in front of potential readers. As I write this, experts estimate there are anywhere from 8 to 40 million books for sale on Amazon, which sells about half of the books purchased in a given year, making it very hard to stand out.

Also, unfortunately, success sometimes triggers anger or jealousy in those closest to us. One of my family members offered lots of encouragement when I struggled to finish and sell my earliest novels. But they began making undermining comments as soon as I got the smallest amount of positive recognition. Those types of remarks escalated the more books I sold. Now it's obvious what's happening, but the negative words made me doubt and question myself.

In addition, writing is personal. Whether you're writing an autobiographical novel or a science fiction action story, you draw on parts of your life and people you know. The more success you have, the more people will be examining those parts of you that are on the page or the screen. Which can also make you feel exposed. And if readers don't like or understand your characters or your story, it can feel like a personal rejection.

Too Much Change

Finishing a novel also causes change. Unless you're a professional writer on a deadline, if you don't finish your novel or publish it you may feel disappointed. But it's likely nothing else in your life will change. Your family, job or career, friends, and hobbies will remain as before.

Success, on the other hand, causes change. Let's say you finish and sell a novel and get a large advance or earn a lot of royalties. At the very least, you'll have more money to deal with. That sounds great, but if you've been in the same financial circumstances for a long time the idea of changing them can bring to mind a whole new set of problems.

Also, you will likely feel pressure to follow up that success with more success. You may start questioning whether the next writing project you have in mind makes sense or will live up to the first one.

Success also can force you to shift priorities. You might need to consider devoting more time to writing and less to some other part of your life. Or it may shift the balance of your relationships.

Not Enough Change

Rather than too much change, you may fear success won't change enough. If you get that large advance or earn a lot of royalties, that won't make everything in your life perfect. In fact, you might discover that your focus on writing your novel allowed you to ignore other problems that now you need to face.

Similarly, if you've been unhappy and thought it was because you hadn't finished your novel or sold it, you may discover that wasn't the issue.

Also, you might sell your novel but still need to work at other jobs or continue earning alternate sources of income. This can be disappointing if you thought that publishing a novel would set you up for good financially.

If you never finish your novel, however, or never to try to sell it, you can keep imagining success will make everything wonderful.

All the above concerns can undermine your drive to finish your novel. You'll need to address them because, and this is the most challenging part, one or all of them will happen. Not making you feel better, right? But I hope it will help to know that there are ways to get past these fears or to write through them, which is what the next chapters are about.

Questions

- Do you identify with any of the concerns this chapter talks about?
- What have you done to deal with them so far?
- Does it make sense that you could fear both success and failure?
- Are you ready to write on and finish your novel anyway?

24

REWRITE AND REDEFINE

Addressing your fears and concerns starts with identifying them. Once you do that, you can search for practical solutions. You can also spot larger underlying issues and deal with them by choosing different words, redefining success and failure, and asking different questions.

Before I get to some ways to do that, an important disclaimer: Sometimes fears or concerns about writing relate to other and deeper issues that may be troubling you. I'm not a therapist or mental health professional. If you struggle with depression, anxiety, or other mental or emotional health issues you may want to seek counseling or therapy.

Okay, let's talk about what's really going on.

Identify What's Happening

Start by getting in touch with your specific concerns about writing a novel. For one writer, it may be revealing too much that's personal. Another may fear discovering that the many hours of writing draw painful comments or negative reviews. Still others may fear being publicly known.

Writing about your concerns can help you sort this out and, as a side benefit, you'll be reinforcing your writing habit. You can free write in a journal, type on your laptop or phone, or speak aloud to yourself or into a recording device. Use the previous chapter to prompt your writing if you need to. Or, if it helps, try starting with a prompt similar to these:

If I spend time writing a novel, I'm afraid that...

If I finish my novel, I am concerned that...

Here's what could happen if I spend a lot time and effort on a novel:

Don't dwell on every uneasy feeling. Just write (or speak) a sentence or two about each concern. Doing this can help you become aware of lurking feelings so you can address them.

_____

_____

_____

_____

_____

_____

_____

_____

_____

_____

_____

_____

_____

_____

_____

Practical Solutions

Most of the specific concerns I listed can be addressed in practical ways. Doing some research on ways to deal with each one may help you move forward.

For example, you'll find that some authors deal with concerns about being stalked or trolled by using pen names. They also get post office boxes so they can avoid using their home addresses for physical mailings, set up separate pen name email addresses, and create entirely separate social media accounts. (One author I know wears a wig and does her make up differently for her author photo, making it that much harder to link her personally to her pen name.)

If you feel like bad reviews will devastate you, you can try reading the most negative reviews of your very favorite books. This can reassure you that those bad reviews didn't hurt the novel's success. Also, compare the negative reviews to the positive ones and notice how often the reviewers comment on the exact same aspect of the book. This helps show you that reviews are much more about reader preferences than whether a novel is objectively "good" or "bad."

If practical solutions, though, don't reassure you, or you find yourself going down endless rabbit holes to address them rather than finishing your novel, your real concern may be less the specific issue and more the overall fears about failing or succeeding.

Either way, the big-picture strategies in the rest of this chapter may help as much or more than looking at specific concerns about issues like bad reviews.

Let's start with considering the words you choose.

Choosing Your Words

Did you notice that rather than fears, I often talk about concerns or issues?

As a writer, you know that words matter, as does what they mean and which words you use. For example, *stride, stalk, stomp,* and *stroll* all conjure different images. They're far more vivid than *walk* because they're more specific, and they tell us something about the person who is walking.

It's just as important to choose and understand the words you use with yourself. The goal isn't to deny your feelings, but to be accurate. Many writers aren't *petrified* or even *afraid* of finishing a novel and being criticized. But most feel a bit *uneasy* about it. Using accurate language can help you write on despite some anxious feelings. And where your concerns rise to the level of fear, you can spend a little more time addressing them.

Look over what you wrote about your fears. Are there words or phrases you used that exaggerated your concerns? If so, go ahead and revise them.

_____

_____

_____

_____

_____

_____

_____

_____

_____

_____

You can also do this type of revision in your mind. If a question or concern occurs to you, try answering it in a toned-down way. For instance, your first answer to the question "What if I spend a year writing this novel and no one buys it?" might be "That would be terrible!" But would it be terrible with an exclamation point? And might it be upsetting or disappointing but not terrible?

You can also change the questions you ask yourself so that you elicit more helpful answers.

New Questions

Review the list of questions at the beginning of Chapter 23. Add any others that spark worries about writing or make you tense.

Now write out different questions, ones designed to get in touch with why you love writing, ways to improve your manuscript, and the benefits of finishing your novel.

For instance, you could ask yourself:

- What part of finishing a novel do I feel most excited about?

- What do I love about spending time writing?
- What three things can I do to make my characters more compelling?
- How can I find ways to increase my chances of selling my novel once I finish it?
- What do I hope readers will like best about my novel?
- What am I excited about writing after I finish this novel?
- How can I put my work out into the world and feel safe doing so?

Each time you begin to dwell on your concerns and issues, you can ask yourself one of these types of questions. It will help redirect your mental energy toward enjoying writing and getting better at it.

Another way to address uneasy feelings also involves words. Specifically, redefining success and failure.

Redefine Your Terms

If you suspect you're struggling with concerns about failing or succeeding, or if you're struggling to finish and aren't sure why, take 10 minutes right now to think about how you define the concepts *failure* and *success* in connection to writing.

As you do, try asking yourself these questions:

- Is there a certain way you want to feel about your work that will tell you if it's a failure or a success?
- Will you feel you've failed if other people dislike or criticize your writing?
- If no more than 50 people buy, download, watch, or read your work, will you feel it's a failure?
- If 50,000 people buy, download, watch, or read it, will that make it a success?
- Does how much money you earn affect success or failure?
- Do you need to feel your writing is the best it can possibly be to decide if it failed or succeeded?

- How do you think you'll react if you feel your writing is a success or failure?
- What do you imagine happening after you finish a writing project?

Now get out your keyboard, grab a sheet of paper, or write in the workbook edition of this book. Spend the next 20 minutes writing as fast as you can in answer to the questions below. Be as specific as you can. Use your thoughts on the above questions if it helps.

- How do you define success in connection with writing?
- How do you define failure in connection with writing?

_____
_____
_____
_____
_____
_____
_____
_____
_____
_____
_____
_____
_____
_____
_____
_____
_____
_____
_____
_____

_____

_____

_____

Now let's talk about whether those definitions are helping you write or may be undermining your efforts.

Shifting The Focus To You

One way to ensure that your definitions of success and failure don't undermine you is to shift your focus to what's within your control. Most of us include in our definitions things that aren't completely in our control, or perhaps aren't in our control at all. For instance, you can influence how many books you sell and how people see your work, but you don't control it. Even if you write a novel that 99% of readers love, the other 1% can still think it's terrible.

That doesn't mean you don't want to sell a certain number of copies or gain positive reviews. Most of us write because we hope that others will read and appreciate our work. But success and failure are big concepts that go far beyond those types of goals. The key is to define both in ways that focus on what's in your control, rings true, and makes it easier to write.

For instance, if you define failure as failing to try something you want to do, then you can choose whether or not you fail because you can choose to try. If you write a novel, any novel, you won't have failed because you tried. (You can still set a goal of selling a certain number of copies or selling to a certain publisher. But you're not calling yourself a success or failure based on achieving those goals.)

Or you can define success at novel writing as delving into topics that matter to you or exploring characters you care about. You can define success as enjoying writing your novel or making space in your life to devote significant time to it.

These are just a few ideas for redefinitions. I'm sure you can think of your own. Look at how you defined success and failure.

Can you revise your definitions to put succeeding or failing within your control?

_____

_____

_____

_____

_____

_____

_____

_____

_____

_____

_____

_____

_____

_____

_____

Finally, you may want to consider whether the concepts of success and failure are helpful at all.

It's All About Results

Whatever you wrote about success and failure, on some level it related to what resulted from the effort, time, and money you put into writing. So why not focus on results? Specifically, you can decide right now that there are no failures or successes, only results. (I've seen this view attributed to many different people, including Tony Robbins, in relation to all aspects of life, not only writing.) This shift helps demystify writing and put it more in line with other pursuits and skills.

Think about it. Almost everything we learn to do involves trying something that doesn't work at all, or as well as we hoped, changing our approach, and trying again. Whether it's learning to walk, swim, ride a bike, or read out loud, most of us need to "fail" many times to learn.

If you watch a baby learning to stand or walk, for example,

you'll see lots of falls and stumbles before that first successful trek across the room. But do we say a 10-month-old baby failed at walking every day until one day the baby "succeeds" at walking? No. We say the baby learned to walk.

For an example related to a creative pursuit, my oldest brother has loved photography all his life. Once I commented that my favorite photos of myself were ones that he took. I asked him how he did it. He said, "You don't see the thousands I throw away."

This was back when all photos were taken on film, meaning he spent money on the film and processing for each one. He could easily have viewed all those thrown-out photos as failures and let that stop him. But if he had, he'd never have produced so many images that made me and many other people happy. He also wouldn't be the excellent photographer he is today. By looking at the results of his efforts, adjusting his approach, and choosing the best photos, he succeeded in his goals.

And as an example from my own life that's specific to writing, in December of 2016 I published a novel, *When Darkness Falls*, in a genre I don't otherwise write in. (Paranormal romance/gothic horror.) When I offer the ebook free it always gets some downloads, but it rarely sells. In fact, it took two years before it earned back what I spent for the cover and the conversion service I used to get the manuscript into ebook format. After that, in all that time I've made only a couple hundred dollars in royalties.

Doesn't sound great, does it? I could consider it a failure.

Instead, I value what I learned from it. As result of writing and publishing it, I figured out how to create a paperback on my own for the first time. It's also the only novel of mine where the digital edition is exclusive to a subscription reading service, so I learned about how that works.

And, my guess is here and there someone reads that book and tries one of my fiction series. Since it costs me nothing to leave *When Darkness Falls* for sale, all sales it prompts of other books are like bonuses. Finally, I wrote that novel before publishing any books, and I learned a lot about novel writing in the process. And that's the best way, in my view, to look at writing a novel, especially your first one.

Everything you write is a building block for your next writing project. If you don't get the results you hoped for this time, you can still learn a lot from it. In fact, you'll probably learn more from what doesn't work than what does. And if you do get the results you want, celebrate, learn what you can, and move on.

Either way you're ahead of the game.

Writing On

Addressing your concerns may not mean they disappear. Most likely they'll occur to you from time to time. You may continue to care deeply what others think of your writing. Or you redefine failure and success but putting your work out there still feels unnerving. Perhaps, like me, you love setting goals and you're apprehensive you'll never meet them.

That's all okay. Now that you're aware of what you're feeling and you've taken some steps to minimize the issues, you can learn to write on anyway. Just as you've likely done many things in life that made you feel a bit nervous.

For instance, I felt nervous my first day, and my next and my next, teaching legal writing at my old law school. But that didn't keep me from doing it, and now teaching's one of my favorite things.

You can do the same with writing, and once you finish your first novel it'll become easier and easier to write no matter what fears you still have.

Here are some steps you can try to help the process along:

- Consider one of the fears you identified. Let yourself feel the apprehension. Maybe your heart beats a little faster. Now take a few minutes to shut your eyes and picture yourself typing, writing in a notebook, or editing your finished draft. This will help ease you into your next writing session.
- Repeat to yourself when it's time to write that you're

only writing a zero draft. Reread the zero draft chapter if you're feeling especially stuck or anxious. Or say out loud, "I'm going to write something bad." I often do this when sitting down to work on a spot in my novel where I feel stuck.

- Practice writing when you feel anxious about it. Start with a journal entry or list of favorite movies if you need to. Get comfortable feeling uneasy and writing all the same. Odds are the feeling will fade. Before you know it you'll be writing your novel or whatever other projects you set your heart on.

- Remind yourself again why you love to write. Review whatever you wrote about why you enjoy novel writing and expand on it. Each time a concern nags at you – such as asking yourself how awful you'll feel if you get a lot of bad reviews – review what you wrote. Reframe every negative question as a positive one that elicits why you want to finish your novel and how excited you are about it.

Last Questions

- What are some things you've done other than writing that you felt nervous about?
- Which question about writing makes you feel the best when you answer it?
- Do your definitions of failure and success keep the focus on you and not on other people?
- What's one thing you can learn from finishing your novel even if the results you get aren't what you hoped for?

L. M. LILLY

_____

_____

_____

_____

_____

_____

_____

_____

_____

_____

_____

_____

25

WHERE DO YOU GO FROM HERE

Wherever you're at in the novel writing process, I hope this book helped you get more in touch with what you love about it. And that the exercises and questions prompt you to dive in, or return to, your novel with renewed excitement. I can't promise there won't ever be moments when writing feels like a slog, or you feel a bit apprehensive when you sit or stand before a blank page. But now you have more tools to know how to fill it up. Plus, understanding what's happening should help ease the tension you feel and help you have more fun as you write on.

For more guidance on plot, time management, character development, or addressing anxiety you might find these books in my Writing As A Second Career series helpful:

- Super Simple Story Structure: A Quick Guide To Plotting And Writing Your Novel
- The One-Year Novelist: A Week-By-Week Guide To Writing Your Novel In One Year
- Creating Compelling Characters From The Inside Out
- How To Write A Novel, Grades 6-8 (if your child wants to try novel writing)

- Buffy And The Art Of Story Season One: Writing Better Fiction By Watching Buffy
- Buffy And The Art Of Story Season Two Part 1: Threats, Lies, and Surprises in Episodes 1-11
- Happiness, Anxiety, And Writing: Using Your Creativity To Live A Calmer, Happier Life

Though I don't currently have courses available on writing or publishing, I find the courses by Joanna Penn of The Creative Penn very helpful and am an affiliate of hers. That means I get a small fee if you sign up for her courses through my link: WritingAsASecond-Career.com/Penn. If you prefer, you can independently search the Internet for her website and courses.

Finally, for help plotting your novel or other fiction, you can get free story structure worksheets at WritingAsASecondCareer.com/Story.

Wishing you luck – and lots of fun – writing your novel!

Did you enjoy this book and find it helpful? Please write a review to help other writers find it, too. Even a sentence or a few words can make a difference.

ABOUT THE AUTHOR

An author, lawyer, and adjunct professor of law, L. M. Lilly's non-fiction includes *Happiness, Anxiety, and Writing: Using Your Creativity To Live A Calmer, Happier Life*; *Super Simple Story Structure: A Quick Guide to Plotting & Writing Your Novel*; and *Creating Compelling Characters From The Inside Out*.

Writing as Lisa M. Lilly, she is the author of the best selling Awakening supernatural thriller series about Tara Spencer, a young woman who becomes the focus of a powerful religious cult when she inexplicably finds herself pregnant, and of the Q.C. Davis suspense/mystery series. She is currently working on the latest book in that series.

Lilly also wrote *When Darkness Falls*, a gothic horror novel set in Chicago's South Loop, and the short-story collection *The Tower Formerly Known as Sears and Two Other Tales of Urban Horror*, the title story of which was made into the short film Willis Tower.

Lilly is a resident of Chicago and a member and past officer of the Alliance Against Intoxicated Motorists. She joined AAIM after an intoxicated driver caused the deaths of her parents in 2007. Her book of essays, Standing in Traffic, is available on AAIM's website.

ALSO BY L. M. LILLY

The One-Year Novelist: A Week-By-Week Guide To Writing Your Novel In One Year

Happiness, Anxiety, and Writing: Using Your Creativity To Live A Calmer, Happier Life

Super Simple Story Structure: A Quick Guide to Plotting and Writing Your Novel

Creating Compelling Characters From The Inside Out

Buffy And The Art Of Story Season One: Writing Better Fiction By Watching Buffy

Buffy And The Art Of Story Season Two Part 1

How To Write A Novel, Grades 6-8

As Lisa M. Lilly:

The Awakening (Book 1 in The Awakening Series)

The Unbelievers (Book 2 in The Awakening Series)

The Conflagration (Book 3 in The Awakening Series)

The Illumination (Book 4 in The Awakening Series)

When Darkness Falls (a standalone supernatural suspense novel)

The Tower Formerly Known As Sears And Two Other Tales Of Urban

Horror

The Worried Man (Q.C. Davis Mystery 1)

The Charming Man (Q.C. Davis Mystery 2)

The Fractured Man (Q.C. Davis Mystery 3)

The Troubled Man (Q.C. Davis Mystery 4)

No Good Plays (A Q.C. Davis Mystery Novella)

Q.C. Davis Mysteries 1-3 (The Worried Man, The Charming Man, and The Fractured Man) Box Set